MENTAL HEALT

Mental Health in Ireland

edited by

Colm Keane

Gill and Macmillan
and
Radio Telefís Éireann

Published by
Gill and Macmillan Ltd
Goldenbridge
Dublin 8
and
Radio Telefís Éireann
Donnybrook
Dublin 4
© The Contributors, 1991
Index compiled by Helen Litton
Print origination by Seton Music Graphics,
Bantry, Co. Cork, Ireland
Printed by Billing & Sons Ltd, Worcester

Contents

List of Contributors

Colm Keane	Senior Journalist and Series Producer, RTE Radio
Anthony Clare	Medical Director, St Patrick's Hospital, Dublin; Clinical Professor of Psychiatry, Trinity College, Dublin
Tom Fahy	Professor of Psychiatry, University College, Galway
Dermot Walsh	Clinical Director, St Loman's Hospital, Dublin
Michael Fitzgerald	Consultant Child Psychiatrist, Eastern Health Board
Frank O'Donoghue	Consultant Psychiatrist, St Patrick's Hospital, Dublin
Margo Wrigley	Consultant Psychiatrist in the Psychiatry of Old Age, James Connolly Memorial Hospital, Dublin
Art O'Connor	Consultant Forensic Psychiatrist, Central Mental Hospital, Dundrum, Dublin
Patrick McKeon	Consultant Psychiatrist, St Patrick's Hospital, Dublin
Marcus Webb	Professor of Psychiatry, Trinity College, Dublin
Charles Smith	Clinical Director, Central Mental Hospital, Dundrum, Dublin; Chairman (Irish Division), Royal College of Psychiatrists

Introduction

Almost every Irish family has had some first-hand experience of mental illness. Forty per cent of illness seen by our general practitioners has a sizeable psychological component. And one out of ten Irish people will at some stage of their lives suffer from a psychiatric disorder. These statistics highlight the extent of mental illness in Ireland today, and it was the size of these figures that prompted RTE Radio to broadcast in the summer of 1990 a series of programmes called 'Mental Health in Ireland'. From the outset it was intended that the series would provide a thoughtful and comprehensive introduction to the central issues of mental health, with the emphasis on the Irish situation. With this in mind, ten psychiatrists were selected to write half-hour papers which would be delivered in lecture form. This would allow the specialist contributors to draw from their impressive clinical and research experience and to deliver a thorough analysis of their areas of specialisation. Some of the topics virtually chose themselves: for example, schizophrenia, depression, alcohol abuse and suicide. Other topics were included, among them the psychiatric problems associated with childhood and with the onset of old age. Further lectures were planned on sexual dysfunction and on the links between crime and mental disorder. It was also decided that the series would include a broad introductory lecture on the question of whether we are indeed 'The Mad Irish', and would conclude with a lecture on the prospects for our mentally ill. The lectures were commissioned specifically for the radio series and were delivered in the Thomas Davis Lecture slot on RTE Radio One.

Nothing could have prepared us for the sheer scale of the problem of mental illness in Ireland, as described by our guest contributors. As the lectures were compiled and broadcast, a grim picture emerged. Dr Patrick McKeon told us of the 200,000 sufferers from depression, the majority of whom carry their pain in private. Dr Dermot Walsh wrote of schizophrenia — which affects one per cent of human populations — and described how many of the victims are 'condemned to a life apart, isolated from gainful employment, from marriage, from friendship . . .'. And what of suicide? Professor Tom Fahy tells us that, '. . . about a thousand [suicide] funerals have taken place up and down this country over the last three years alone — that is, at least one each day — and upwards of 20,000 Irish people have lost a loved one through suicide in the last ten years.' Professor Marcus Webb continued the litany of suffering, this time from alcohol abuse. As he explains, 'We use alcohol for celebration and for softening sorrows, for relaxation and to give courage, for cementing commercial agreements and for loosening artistic expression.' Hardly surprising then that in recent years 'alcoholism and alcoholic psychoses formed the commonest reason for admission to psychiatric hospital . . . ahead of depression and schizophrenia'.

Turning to the psychiatry of childhood, where can one find more disturbing evidence than from Dr Michael Fitzgerald, who describes how, when nine- to eleven-year-olds in disadvantaged areas were asked if life was worth living, 15 per cent thought it was not most of the time and a further 18 per cent thought it wasn't worth living some of the time. Nor do many of our old-aged fare better. Dr Margo Wrigley tells us about the common problem of dementia — with its 20,000 to 30,000 sufferers — which will become 'increasingly more common because of the trend for people to live longer'. And what about sexuality? Dr Frank O'Donoghue turned to the records of the Psycho-Sexual Clinic at St Patrick's Hospital and analysed the non-consummated marriages, the sufferers of low sex drive and painful intercourse, the sexually deviant and the sexually ignorant. He says, '. . . if one were asked to make an educated guess at the prevalence of dysfunction, one would hazard at around 20 per cent of the general population.'

Finally to crime, where Dr Art O'Connor describes how the schizophrenic, the depressed or even the disordered personality can turn to a range of crimes from sexual violence and rape, to exhibitionism and paedophilia, even homicide.

As the lectures were presented, it was impossible to avoid concluding just how incomplete our understanding is of mental disorder and how misunderstood are our mentally ill. As Professor Anthony Clare put it, 'The result of public fear, ignorance, prejudice and withdrawal is stigma: the mentally ill are marked and branded as fearsome, evil, inferior, weak, dangerous, unpredictable, unreliable and, by the particularly ignorant, contagious.' But there are also hopes for the future, new policy directives involving a more caring approach and more community support. Yet how disturbing it is to hear Dr Charles Smith describe how he visited the hostels for the homeless only to find the presence of deinstitutionalised patients, unable to function outside the asylum walls. Dr Smith says, 'We are at a crossroads now and we need to stop and read the signposts . . . as we push an inadequately funded service, that affects so many individuals and families, toward an uncertain future.'

The lectures printed in the following pages are not a definitive study of mental illness in Ireland, nor do they pretend to be. The limitations of broadcast time forced us to bypass many issues that could have been covered if the space were available. Perhaps the areas of drug-dependence, anxiety, stress, phobias and panic attacks will receive appropriate treatment in the future. Similarly, in many cases the lack of statistical evidence prevented any clearcut statements or analyses to be made on the prevalence of certain disorders in the Irish context. Ultimately, however, it is hoped that the lectures will contribute to a better understanding of the causes of mental breakdown and lead to a greater tolerance of the mentally ill. If the lectures should go even partly to achieving this goal, the work involved will have been worthwhile.

Colm Keane

ONE

The Mad Irish?

Anthony Clare

In the mid–1960s when I was working in the United States, I mentioned to one of my senior colleagues there that I intended to return to Ireland to become a psychiatrist. He responded in astonishment: 'Surely Ireland doesn't need psychiatrists?' His idea of Ireland as a tranquil, harmonious land, its people content and Catholic, its villages and towns havens of stability and social grace, cohabited uneasily with the notion of psychiatry and its implications of depression and disaster, psychopathology and pain. It is, in truth, a continuing contrast. On the one hand we Irish do think of our native land as a reasonably stable place, the Northern troubles notwithstanding. The great majority of our people share the same social background, the same ethnic origin, the same religious faith. We have been spared awesome war, serious poverty and civil upheaval for over half a century. And yet, we still boast (if that is the word) a large mental hospital in virtually every sizeable town, from Castlebar to Ardee, from Killarney to Monaghan. The average Irishman's chances of spending some time in a psychiatric hospital for the treatment of alcohol abuse, for example, are higher than virtually any of his European neighbours. Until recently, the Irish were thought to be particularly prone to schizophrenia. That no longer appears so, but just as we breathed a sigh of relief attention has turned to our rates of manic-depression. We Irish do indeed appear to be particularly prone to experiencing marked and pathological swings of mood, otherwise known as manic-depressive illness. And there is suicide, called by some Ireland's greatest secret; for example, the rate of suicide increased six times in the fifteen years from 1970 to 1985, and every week between twelve and fifteen people kill themselves in Ireland.

Yet some of this dramatic excess of mental ill-health may be more apparent than real. Ireland does have a large number of psychiatric hospitals and has done ever since the extraordinary boom in asylum building which occurred throughout the Western world during the nineteenth century. Historians still argue about the causes of this development, some emphasising the effect of urbanisation on the difficulty of maintaining the mentally ill in the community; others suggesting that there had developed a greater awareness of the problem of mental ill-health. Others argue that, with the decline of rural communities and the break-up of the extended family, the mentally ill became more and more the responsibility of the State and local authorities. Whatever the explanation, the numbers of people in mental asylums rose dramatically during the latter half of the 1800s. For example, in 1851 there were just over 10,000 people in Irish mental hospitals out of a population of 6.5 million. By 1901 there were 25,000 inpatients out of a population of 4.5 million! The number of inpatients remained at or around 20,000 well into the 1960s when it began to fall. Now, as we move towards the end of the twentieth century, the number of psychiatric inpatients has moved back towards what it was 150 years ago: about 8,500, although, of course, the population today is less than half of what it was when the asylum building programme first took off!

So, one explanation as to why so many Irish people have been in mental hospitals could be that we had mental hospitals and had to fill them with somebody. But what, therefore, of the high rate of schizophrenia which supposedly afflicts us? For some years now Irish family life patterns, dominant mothers, religious scrupulosity, the fear of sexuality and the value placed on supernatural phenomena have all been blamed as the cause of Irish schizophrenia. One noted psychiatric researcher, H.B.M. Murphy, even went so far as to suggest that Irish verbal skills, most notably our penchant for double-talk, ambiguity and obfuscation, may create intolerable levels of tension which could lead to schizophrenia in predisposed individuals. The fertility of the explanations offered has been reduced somewhat by the finding recently, by Dermot Walsh and his colleagues at the Medico-Social Research Board, that in fact Irish rates of schizophrenia are *not* excessive by international standards; a case of wonderfully attractive theories being slaughtered by a single, dampening fact!

What is unarguable is our national problem with alcohol. But even here there are contradictions. The amount of alcohol drunk per capita is the second lowest in Europe. Yet the proportion of our personal disposable income that we spend on alcohol is one of the highest in Europe. A remarkable proportion of the Irish population, about 20 per cent, drinks no alcohol at all, while perhaps as many as one in ten drinks himself to disease and even death. Such findings reflect the clinical impression that attitudes to alcohol in Ireland are hopelessly ambivalent and oscillate between stern disapproval and permissive indulgence.

Irish society has long been accused of an over-indulgence towards heavy drinking and intoxication. In a classic account of the cultural value of Irish drinking, Bales observed that 'the man who is drunk is sometimes regarded with envy by the man who is sober'. Another popular cultural explanation is that which invokes the efficacy of alcohol in suppressing sexual feelings and drive. Irish society has featured strong sexual taboos and, for some men at least, drinking may well be a satisfactory and tolerated substitute for unwanted sexual behaviour. Indeed, Arensberg claimed that lower middle-class Irishmen in the first half of this century regarded the teetotaller as a menace to society because he was seen to be the man most likely to prowl the streets getting the girls into trouble. Arensberg argued that 'any emotional difficulty is believed best treated by advising them to drink it off. Drowning one's sorrows becomes the expected means of relief, much as a prayer among the women and younger children, or among the older people.' Bales drew attention to the words of *Cruiskeen Lawn* and points out that they can be seen as a reflection of the function of drinking as a sexual substitute. The words of the chorus translated into English are, 'The love of my heart is my little full jug, here's health to the darling girl'.

So: a large number of psychiatric beds, but falling; an apparent excess of schizophrenia, now regarded as not particularly significant; a definite problem with alcohol; what else can be said about Irish mental health? Our rates of mood disorder — illnesses such as depression and manic-depressive disorder — do seem high. This has also led to a plethora of explanations, some environmental, some genetic. The most compelling cultural explanation has been that which points to the impact of centuries of foreign political and psychological domination on the Irish mind, a mind enveloped and to an extent suffocated in an English mental embrace. Professor Joseph Lee's monumental historical exploration of the evolution of modern Ireland refers to what he calls 'the elusive but crucial psychological factors that inspired the instinct of inferiority' and 'shrivelled Irish perspectives on Irish potential'. He was writing of Irish political development but his words are applicable to the individual Irish psyche. We are given to gloomy self-doubt, we lack self-esteem, we exude guilt, self-reproach, futility: the cardinal characteristics of depression.

Before continuing further and exploring some of these theories, before considering, for example, Michael Kelleher's finding that we Irish are more obsessional and anxious than our nearest English neighbours, I should perhaps confront a very common Irish, and indeed universal,

objection to statements about the prevalence of mental
illness. At the end of the day, sure aren't we all a little
mad? Is not the very definition of mental illness itself
hopelessly subjective? Is not one man's madness another
man's eccentricity? And what of the claim, currently highly
popular, which asserts that the most creative members of
society, the writers, painters, poets, dramatists, musicians,
sculptors, the most energetic businessmen, politicians,
architects, philosophers, mathematicians, contain within
their ranks a significant number of people who would be
diagnosed mentally ill by psychiatrists such as myself? What
about, objects the critic, warming to his theme, Brendan
Behan, Eugene O'Neill, Ernest Hemingway, John Donne,
Gerard Manley Hopkins, Sylvia Plath, Virginia Woolf,
Robert Lowell, Malcolm Lowry, Ezra Pound, Auguste
Strindberg, Leo Tolstoy, Samuel Johnson, Peter Tchai-
kovsky, Robert Schumann, Joseph Conrad — just some of
the artists who have been regarded as having problems
with alcohol, with drugs, with mental illness or indeed
with all three?

Pausing merely to observe that having a mental illness
is no more a bar to being highly intelligent, remarkably
talented, wondrously gifted and a boon to society and civilisation than suffering from epilepsy, disseminated sclerosis,
diabetes or TB, let me explain. A diagnosis of mental
illness usually means in practice that:

(*a*) a person is experiencing symptoms characteristically
regarded as psychological, such as anxiety, depression,
elation, hallucinations, delusions, obsessions, compulsions;

(*b*)   the symptoms are severe and disabling; that is to
say, the individual is distressed by them, cannot function,
feels 'unwell'. The layman's term is 'breakdown' and it is a
good one for it suggests that the individual's normal ability
to cope with stress or setback has broken down, that he or
she has lost the normal ability to ease tension, lift mood,
regain control, cope;

(*c*) the individual is so afflicted that he or she cannot ordinarily recover control without external help, be it by means of talking and listening and learning (psychotherapy, behaviour therapy), physical treatment (drugs, ECT) and/ or social interventions (attention to stresses at work, in the home, within marriage or relating to money, status, power);

(*d*) the ill-health can be caused by genetic factors; by loss, such as bereavement or unemployment or financial disaster; by catastrophic stress such as war, disasters like the Lockerbie air tragedy or the Stardust fire; by physical illness; or, indeed, a combination of some or all of these factors. Rarely is there a single cause of a psychiatric illness and rarely, too, a single treatment.

Most patients recognise they are unwell and seek treatment. Out of 2,500 patients admitted to St Patrick's Hospital in 1989 only 110 were compulsorily admitted, that is to say, against their will.

None the less, it will be objected, why should anyone be so coerced? After all, physically ill patients, despite being obviously ill, even dying, can refuse treatment, take their own discharge and die if they so wish; why should mentally ill individuals lose their autonomy, their civil rights, their freedom? It is an awesome issue and it revolves around an assumption which can be traced back to the earliest civilisations, that there are certain illnesses which by their very nature impair our minds to the extent of affecting our judgment, our very reason. At the extremes there are rarely such problems: the individual who, under the influence of a drug like LSD or alcohol, insists he can fly and tries to do so out of an eighth-floor window, is usually seen as in need of restraint and detoxification. The profoundly suicidal depressed patient who insists, against all the evidence, that he has committed some appalling crime or is rotting with cancer or is spreading the world with AIDS is again usually seen as someone for whom protection and treatment are indicated; particularly since recovery from such a state is well-nigh guaranteed. The problem arises when the mental disturbance is less clear cut and the individual insists that far from being out of control he or she is completely responsible. There are problems, too, when experiences which in one culture are seen as unusual but normal are seen in another culture as symptoms of a severe mental illness: the experience of demoniacal possession, for example, or the conviction that one has magical powers of mind-reading.

The great bulk of psychiatrists, in common with legislators, lawyers and philosophers, recognise the problems. For that reason the law circumscribing the powers of psychiatrists has been strengthened in many countries in recent years to protect individuals from being hospitalised against their will in all but the most serious circumstances *and* to protect the mentally ill individual's right to receive psychiatric treatment of an appropriate quality and standard should his/her mental state require it. Modern mental health legislation emphasises the individual's speedy access to an appeals tribunal in the event of compulsory hospitalisation, such a tribunal containing representatives of the law and the general public as well as psychiatry. It also carefully delineates the circumstances in which compulsory hospitalisation and treatment can legally be employed and the restrictions on such power. At the present time mental health legislation in Ireland has lagged behind such developments; there have been a number of attempts to modernise our mental health legislation in the light of modifications in other parts of the world, and such modernisation is, in my view, long overdue. That having been said, there is little evidence that psychiatric powers in this country are being abused. But as in so much else, it is important that not only should justice be done, it should be seen to be done.

My emphasis on serious mental illnesses, such as suicidal depression, severe alcohol abuse, schizophrenia, together with my references to mental hospitals and psychiatrists, should not blind people to one important fact about psychological ill-health, namely, that it is spread across a spectrum of severity and that much of it, indeed the bulk of it, is seen and treated not by psychiatrists but by general practitioners. It is the average GP who sees the great bulk of depressions, anxiety attacks, panics and phobias, stress-related disorders; perhaps as many as one in every seven people attending their GP is there largely or entirely for psychiatric reasons. And much of the illnesses seen by hospital physicians, by gynaecologists, rheumatologists, cardiologists are also psychological in origin or are physical conditions aggravated by psychological factors. Many conditions are perhaps best conceived of as neither physical nor psychological but an inextricable mixture of both. Many so-called alternative therapists or holistic therapists (therapists who emphasise the importance of relaxation, diet, exercise, healthy living and attention to the environment) are in the best tradition of Hippocrates, the father of Western medicine, who regarded all illness as affecting to a greater or lesser extent our minds and bodies. The message for contemporary scientific medicine would appear clear: the diagnosis and management of a wide variety of illnesses — depression and disseminated sclerosis, Parkinson's disease and premenstrual tension, stroke and schizophrenia, cancer and colitis, diabetes and drug dependence, AIDS and anxiety attacks — require attention to the individual's mental as well as physical function.

But such an integrated view, which underpinned medicine until the late seventeenth century, is not easy to hold. Physicians are often dismissive of psychological factors, while the patient is nervous of any suggestion of psychological involvement in his or her ill-health. For some explanations of this we need to return to the rise of the mental hospital in the early nineteenth century mentioned earlier. People have always been anxious about mental illness; after all, it implies a loss of control in the one area that determines our essential humanity, namely, our mind. That is a legitimate reason for anxiety, and if it were the only one I feel sure we could confront and combat it. But it is not the only worry. Mental illness is also associated with features of the mental hospital: it is hidden away behind walls, it seems to be incurable because, in the early days at any rate, few of the people who went into the local mental asylum ever seemed to come out; it appears to be dangerous (why else would patients be locked away from sight and sound?). Mental illness is seen to reflect badly on the sufferer: he or she is regarded as morally weak, spiritually deficient (shades here of accusations of witchcraft and evil possession) or physically defective. Sufferers from mental illness not surprisingly keep their experiences to themselves. Whereas sufferers from diabetes or heart disease or asthma or even AIDS seem able to 'come out' as it were, and speak publicly of their illnesses and their treatment and, where relevant, of their recovery, patients who have been depressed or manic or highly anxious or addicted remain silent for fear of discrimination at work, in clubs and societies, in their village or town or city. The media do not always help. Every strange violent act, involving a mass murder like Hungerford or a mass murderer like Charles Manson, is the signal for an immense and usually ill-informed series of speculations concerning the link between mental illness and violence, thereby reinforcing the public's erroneous view of the mentally ill as a group particularly predisposed to antisocial and, especially, violent behaviour.

The result of public fear, ignorance, prejudice and with-drawal is stigma: the mentally ill are marked and branded as fearsome, evil, inferior, weak, dangerous, unpredictable, unreliable and, by the particularly ignorant, contagious. Our use of psychiatric terminology reflects our prejudice and ignorance. Time and again people who should know better, politicians for example, use the term 'schizophrenic' as one of abuse and they use it inaccurately. Terms like 'psycho' (and indeed the film of that name) reinforce notions of dangerousness and almost animal-like aberration. One consequence is that some patients would almost prefer a diagnosis of an untreatable, fatal physical disease than of a treatable psychiatric disorder on account of a vague feeling that mental illness is not 'true' illness.

Such notions are slowly giving way as people become more educated and informed about mental health and illness. More and more individuals in public life who have suffered from mental ill-health are prepared to talk openly about it. In Britain a diverse group of people including the comedian Spike Milligan, the pianist John Ogdon, a former President of the Royal College of General Practitioners, Dr John Horder, and the novelist Susan Hill have openly talked of their psychiatric illnesses and have been joined in this country by, amongst others, singer Johnny McEvoy and the Oscar-winner Brenda Fricker. How long, though, will we have to wait in Ireland for a politician to reveal he or she has had a psychiatric disorder akin to British Home Secretary, David Waddington's revelation that he suffered a depressive disorder in 1974? There are signs of a breakthrough: most people seem quite willing to admit to suffering from stress — indeed, it has been said that 'stress' is the one fashionable psychiatric disorder — so it may only be a matter of time before we can as a species admit that from time to time many of us, perhaps most of us, undergo a period of mental distress sufficiently severe, lengthy and uncontrollable as to warrant the description 'illness'. The media, blamed earlier by me for stigmatising the mentally ill and reinforcing prejudice and fear, can play and are beginning to play a vitally important role in educating the public about the realities of mental illness and psychiatric treatment. Television documentaries, soap operas, newspaper articles and exposés, magazine interviews with therapists and patients, theatrical and cinematic portrayals of mental illness can and do undermine public ignorance and indifference and redirect public attention and resources towards a hitherto neglected area of need.

This process of de-stigmatisation could be accelerated by the run-down of the large mental hospital and its replacement by a system of psychiatric care composed of smaller psychiatric units attached to general hospitals, supporting and supported by a variety of facilities and resources in the community, including hostels, sheltered workshops, day hospitals and centres and a variety of skilled professionals — social workers, psychologists, community psychiatric nurses, occupational therapists — deployed to help those who have always borne and still bear the greatest burden in the provision of care for the mentally ill, namely, the relatives. But, if the run-down of the psychiatric hospitals occurs without a simultaneous development of such community-based care — which is what many of us fear may be happening — public hostility towards and fear of psychiatric patients could actually be exacerbated by the sight of many chronically ill people wandering the streets, caught up in petty crime, and sleeping rough.

Failure to develop an appropriate system of hospital- and community-based psychiatric care would merely mean replacing one deficient system of diagnosis and treatment by another. It would also mean that we could continue to ignore the implications of mental ill-health for our society. As long as mental illness is out of sight and out of mind we do not need to consider those aspects of our society that might exacerbate our normal human tendency to mental ill-health. Out of sight and mind, mental illness can continue to receive a miserable and inadequate proportion of the health budget and can languish at the bottom of the league table when it comes to research monies and resources.

How far we have been protected by this process, I suspect, can be gauged by the lack of impact consideration of our levels of mental health and illness have exercised on our assessments of the quality of Irish life. Discussions, for example, about Irish marriage and family life do not always reflect the reality seen in the Irish psychiatric clinic: our emphasis on marital stability or the seeming decency of family life ignores the appalling toll taken of intimate relationships by alcohol abuse and the tensions, manipulations and even abuse which occur behind closed domestic doors. There has been an uneasy silence concerning the psychological price paid by many of our religious for celibacy, a striking lack of psychological analysis of our penchant for intemperateness of which Yeats wrote the memorable lines:

> Out of Ireland have we come,
> Great hatred, little room,
> Maimed us at the start.
> I carry from my mother's womb
> A fanatic heart.

Reference to Yeats serves to remind me of the fact that it has been Irish writers who have filled the vacuum of psychological analysis and have charted and documented the moulds and the impressions left on the Irish psyche by a culture heavily impregnated by an emphasis on physical control, original sin, cultural inferiority and psychological defensiveness. So neglected have the psychological aspects of Irish life remained that when an otherwise excellent collection of essays appeared under the title *The Irish Mind* there were sections devoted to the philosophical, political, scientific and even literary aspects of the elusive Irish psyche, but a psychological section there was not!

Such psychological and psychiatric analyses as there have been have, as one might expect, been critical. A child psychiatrist writing in 1976 on discipline in the Irish family commented:

The family home in Ireland is a novitiate for violence. Even from the cradle the child is made to feel rejection, hostility and open physical pain. The infant is left to cry in his cot because his mother does not want to 'give in to him'. Later he is smacked with the hand or a stick.

He is made to go to bed early. He is not allowed to have his tea. He is put into a room by himself . . . and in order to invite this morale-breaking treatment from his parents, all the Irish child has to do is to be *normal*. It is the normality of childhood which sets parents' teeth on edge. They take no joy in childishness.

Noel Browne, himself a psychiatrist, has reflected on the role played by fear in Irish child-rearing practices and has observed that it can and often does simply lead

to a practice of deceit by the child of the parents, of other adults and especially of the teacher. In manner, the child pretends to conform while the threat of punishment exists, or else he simply learns to deceive and lie to avoid the distress of punishment.

Now others — historians, philosophers, political analysts — have mused on the Irish ability to say one thing and do another; but there is a psychology, too, of such behaviour and a corresponding need to explore it. But, like the exploration of a patient, it needs sensitivity if it is not further to damage self-esteem and feed our tendency to self-denigration. Too much time in the psychiatric clinic can lead to the blinkered conclusion that Irish family life is scarred and distorted by threats and compulsions: the use of humiliation and silence to control; powerful, possessive Irish mothers investing sons with all the wild and unrealistic hopes which passive husbands have failed to fulfil; guilt-ridden sons, burdened by such unasked-for crosses and threatened by a sexuality portrayed as animalistic when expressed outside marriage and sacred when expressed within it; and Irish daughters crippled by an ideal of adulthood which appears to blend the somewhat irreconcilable realities of virginity and motherhood; the resulting mixture stewed in a potent brew of religiosity, guilt and alcohol.

But psychiatry is about strengths too, and it can be anticipated that the emergence of mental illness from the isolated mental hospitals to which it has for so long been banished will result in light being focussed on the extra-ordinary vigour and vitality of so much of Irish life, the resilience of families and friends in the face of mental and physical deprivation, the decency and cohesiveness of so much that is Irish social life, the genuine constancy and commitment to children and elderly, to the lonely and the lost, which are an intimate part of life on this island. Psychiatry, it has been said, reminds us of the essential ambiguity and contradictoriness of human life. A greater understanding of mental ill-health, of our own precarious stability, of the stresses and strains that can break any and all of us, of the defences we have erected to help us cope and which occasionally actually prevent us from growing, that understanding ultimately could help make life here (and perhaps elsewhere) a little more fulfilled, satisfying, dare one say it, happier. That greater understanding will only come with a greater honesty about our mental life now. It is towards that greater understanding that this series of lectures is aimed.

TWO

Suicide and the Irish: from sin to serotonin

Tom Fahy

To attend the funeral of a friend or relative who has committed suicide is an unforgettable experience: the shocked disbelief, the muted sermon, the silence at the graveyard, the house private and the most un-Irish isolation of the family in their grief. If the latest published figures on Irish suicides are even halfway correct, about a thousand such funerals have taken place up and down this country over the last three years alone — that is, at least one each day — and upwards of 20,000 Irish people have lost a loved one through suicide in the last ten years.

In common with other Western countries, official suicide rates have been rising steeply over the last twenty years, the increase being about fourfold since 1968 and most marked in young people. For example, recorded suicides averaged about sixty per year in the 1960s, rising steeply to nearly 300 by the end of 1988. Below thirty years of age the numbers increased most dramatically, from a handful only to begin with, by a factor of over 1,000 per cent. This very dramatic increase has been noticed by World Health Organisation scientists, one of whom recently characterised Ireland as the 'nation most at risk' for the accelerating suicide of its young people. If these figures shock you, as well they might, it may help to trace briefly the 'black thread' of suicide in history. It is a grim story.

From time immemorial, self-homicide, *felo de se*, or *feinmharbhu* has existed. Suicide recurs frequently in Greek and Norse mythology. In Irish mythology, Deirdre threw herself into her lover's grave; and the death of Cuchulain, who went into his last battle knowing he had lost his magic powers, was self-sacrificial, to say the least. The ancient Greeks, like their gods, took a cool and rational approach to suicide but they were not permissive. In ancient Athens, the bodies of suicide victims were buried outside the walls, the right hand severed and buried separately. The Romans took life more cheaply and their approach was more businesslike. Roman citizens could get permission of the Senate to take their own lives but this was denied to slaves and criminals on economic grounds. Orthodox religions which value the sanctity of life have generally condemned suicide but in varying degrees. The traditional Christian proscription is by far the most severe. It dates from earliest times, although the four suicides of the Old Testament — Samson's being the most famous — and that of Judas in the New Testament were never explicitly condemned by the Scripture writers. Unsympathetic historians suggest that the Christian ethic evolved as a reaction to the 'suicide mania' of some early Christians in their desire for quick martyrdom. Be that as it may, steadily from St Augustine onwards, theological condemnation gained in strength, and by the end of the seventh century both suicide and attempted suicide were firmly condemned as the gravest of mortal sins for which there could be no forgiveness.

We may not assume from this that St Patrick's approach to the fifth-century Irish was equally censorious. Patrick, Ciaran and the others encountered a Gaelic civilisation which was rural, hierarchical and family oriented. Fergus Kelly states that in early Irish law, suicide was classified as a form of kin slaying or *fingal* and therefore a most horrendous form of unlawful killing. Civil penalties included forfeiture of goods to abbot or king. Suicide gets little mention in the old law texts, however, and it is tempting to speculate that among the early native Irish it was genuinely rare.

In the expanding world of Christendom, anti-suicide theology was quickly incorporated into civil legislation, and for more than a thousand years after St Augustine the suicidal and their families were systematically ostracised and persecuted on a grand scale. The original charitable intentions of Augustine had somehow gone terribly wrong. The association between suicide, crime and sin did not weaken until the late seventeenth century when, bit by bit, legal penalties fell away, mainly by default. The literary critic, Alvarez, adduces much evidence that suicide was widely discussed in Elizabethan England when 'melancholia' (as it was then understood) was not so much a disease as a fashionable post-Renaissance pose adopted by poets, painters and playwrights. John Donne, the Anglican priest and poet, wrote *Biothanatos* as a young man, but later as Dean of St Paul's he was ashamed of it and it was not published until after his death and against his wishes. Robert Burton's *The Anatomy of Melancholy* contained an eloquent plea for sympathy towards the depressed melancholic. Burton, himself a depressive who eventually hanged himself, wrote in English and his book was widely read. Shakespeare crammed fourteen suicides into eight of his tragedies. Shakespearean suicides tend to be either ennobling (such as Othello's), romantic (such as Romeo's) or merely pitiable (such as Ophelia's), but never scandalous. Hamlet's soliloquies on the subject were, one imagines, received with rapt attention by packed audiences at least until the Puritans closed the theatres in 1642.

By contrast to Britain and mainland Europe, we encounter complete silence on the subject at this time in Ireland. Why is this? Could it be that these aspects of our mythology and folklore were censored by monkish scribes? Between them, the ecclesiastic and civil authorities had complete control of the written media. The English tradition of vernacular drama was not matched by the Irish for 300 years. Native Irish drama — if such there was — was subsumed in the Bardic oral tradition, in the wandering poets and *seanchai* whose language was scholastic and whose voices grew weaker as English became the language of the common Irish people. The Irish are not heard to mention suicide until Yeats's Deirdre of the Sorrows sells her soul to the devil, and even then, the story was received with much grumbling in the stalls of the Abbey Theatre.

To take the story further we are again forced to look abroad briefly. By 1700 in England, and presumably in Ireland too, legal if not ecclesiastic attitudes had softened. Legal sanctions — such as desecration of the corpse, denial of burial in consecrated ground, and forfeiture of goods to the State — were being sidestepped by an increasingly sympathetic judiciary by the device of bringing verdicts of suicide 'whilst the balance of the mind was disturbed'. This change of heart was slow, however. As recently as 1823 a Mr Griffiths was buried at a crossroads in Chelsea, a stake through his heart, and hanging for attempted suicide was recorded in London up to 1860. Even after that the bodies of pauper suicides were dissected in anatomy departments for fifty years. In Ireland, denial of burial in consecrated ground may be within the memory of our more senior citizens. The year of 1990 is the two-hundredth anniversary of the final abolition of legal penalties for suicide and attempted suicide in Revolutionary France, but it was not until a mere thirty years ago that the British Suicide Act of 1961 saw Britain follow suit, and even then severe penalties for incitement to suicide have been retained, and a coroner's verdict of suicide still needs the full force of legal proof. In Ireland, the common law prohibition of suicide has never been repealed.

With the takeover of the mental asylums by the medical alienists in the nineteenth century, mental illness as a basis for many suicides became a topic for discussion at medical meetings. However, these early psychiatrists' views were drowned out at the end of the nineteenth century by the voice of the great French sociologist, Emile Durkheim. Durkheim believed that vulnerability to suicide depended on the strength of bonds between the individual and society: the weaker these bonds the greater the risk. To further his sociological theories, Durkheim rather mischievously ignored the protestations of early psychiatrists that mental illness had an important part to play in many cases. He noted an increased incidence in the aged, the infirm and the isolated, and in industrialised areas such as inner cities where in Europe at least — if not in Ireland — the cohesion of society was at its weakest. His influence conspired to shift the blame for suicide away from the individual and towards society itself.

Serious attention to the individual psychology of suicide — without the intrusion of spiritual, philosophical or legal considerations — had to await the indepth psychology of Sigmund Freud and his followers in the early part of this century. Freudian psychoanalysis focussed on the individual once more but this time in a decidedly medical context. The devastation of the First World War influenced Freud to postulate an unconscious death instinct in all of us, which he called *Thanatos*, to account not only for individual suicide but also for the apparent universal bent of the human race towards violent self-destruction. In general, psychoanalytic attempts to explain suicide have not gained wide acceptance.

The literary philosopher, Albert Camus, wrote his famous essay on suicide, *The Myth of Sisyphus*, around 1940, with Europe again in the throes of war. He began: 'There is but one truly serious philosophical problem and that is suicide.' Camus was fascinated with the very rarity of suicide given the apparent meaninglessness of life and its absurd quality for so many people. He was, of course, writing at the dawn of scientific psychiatry and just before the introduction of effective treatment for severe depressive illness. Yet Camus poses a question which medical scientists are still struggling to answer: just why do people commit suicide?

Even in high suicide countries, self-homicide is a rare event and correspondingly hard to predict. The modern view is that victims are caught in the cross-fire between serious mental illness on the one hand, and extreme personal vulnerability at a point of time, on the other. Contrary to popular belief, the suicidal state of mind is not something which persists over weeks or even days: the impulse comes on suddenly and does not last for long. Severe depressive illness brings with it psychological effects which distort perception. Very depressed people feel worthless and alone even in the midst of family and friends. The illness can cause extreme anguish, and in this setting successful suicide becomes almost understandable.

However, not all suicides have major depressive illness, especially when the victim is young, and it is amongst the young that suicide rates are rising most quickly. If one recalls that the child's idea of death is one of a temporary adventure, childish remarks such as 'you'll be sorry when I'm dead' are not reasons for great alarm in parents. But this kind of magical thinking can persist into adulthood in persons who fail to mature and who suffer from chronic lack of confidence. Such individuals are over-represented amongst those who attempt suicide. The ambivalence of young suicide victims about death as a terminal event is reflected in remarks, threats and notes which are often worded in such a way as to give the impression that the victim expects to be a witness at the discovery of his own body and looks forward to the consternation of the finders. It is this quality of resentment and hostility in pre-suicide communications which confers so much guilt and frustration on family survivors and makes it so difficult for them to come to terms with suicidal death.

Nowadays rational intellectual suicide, beloved of moral philosophers and a feature of older civilisations, no doubt occurs but is rare in this part of the world. The majority of cases are now seen as problems for medical scientists and needing support and care rather than censure. Vulnerability increased by chronic debilitating illness; single or divorced men over fifty-five years are most at risk, and drug or alcohol abuse may facilitate the act. Lack of a strong personal philosophy of the sanctity of human life combined with instability of personality also weakens resistance.

Suicide seldom occurs completely out of the blue. Warnings are given, threats made and notes left. Nobody is left untouched. There is a tendency for suicides to run in families but this may have as much to do with cultural suppression of mourning in family survivors as with any element of genetic inheritance. Because the act of suicide is surrounded by so much intense emotion, it is not surprising that society has constantly looked for a scapegoat. The blame, first attributed to sin, then to crime and then to society had by the mid-twentieth century shifted again, this time in the direction of mental illness. Suicide was now a public health problem, scientifically respectable and a suitable case for treatment. A new medical industry, 'suicidology', was born.

Systematic collection of national statistics on suicide began in earnest in the nineteenth-century. A trend for rates to rise was noticed early on. The *Encyclopaedia Britannica* of 1911 noted this with concern and drew attention to excessive rates in men, the old, the single and the lonely. It was soon realised that national statistics generally underestimated the size of the problem. Even today, under-reporting is acknowledged to be widespread. The extent of this 'concealment' varies with national systems of recording and certifying of death and also with the strength of local taboo against the public declaration of suicide as a mode of death. This taboo is thought to be greater in Roman Catholic countries like Ireland, but the connection does not always hold, as evidenced by Hungary, a Catholic country with a high suicide rate. Despite the unreliability of national statistics, differences in rates *between* countries have been remarkably consistent. This inter-country rank order is maintained by emigrants from Europe to both Australia and the US and may persist in the adopted country for up to two generations. This remarkable finding is taken as evidence that national culture has a powerful effect on the incidence of suicide.

Ireland has always declared one of the lowest suicide rates in the world and has been constantly suspected of concealment. We have the doubtful distinction of being one of the few Christian countries left where legal sanctions against suicide persist in common law: suicide is a felony, attempted suicide a misdemeanour. This has the effect that our statistics do not derive directly from coroners. Irish coroners are constrained from returning a verdict of suicide by the Coroners Act of 1962 which forbids them to either attribute blame or to exonerate in matters of civil or criminal liability. To get around this, since 1967 confidential police reports are supplied to our Central Statistics Office after inquests on deaths suspected of being unnatural. These reports are doubtless influenced by the individual garda's opinion as to whether the case was one of suicide or not. The precise manner by which final decisions about suicide as a mode of death are made have not so far been publicly declared. Research by Irish psychiatrists in the 1970s and 1980s suggest that the official Irish rate might need to be multiplied by two or three to arrive at a true rate.

The recent steep rise in Irish suicide rates noted earlier dates from the introduction of the new confidential police form in 1967. It was also at this time that the coding of 'undetermined' was introduced for the first time to accommodate the many cases where the suicidal mode of death cannot be decided with certainty. This change of coding practice makes it possible that some at least of the increase in Irish rates may owe more to better reporting than to a real increase. But the rise in suicide rates has not been paralleled by any corresponding drop in 'undetermined' deaths. This ominous fact makes it more likely that the rise is indeed real and not due merely to new coding practices or better reporting. These uncertainties may be resolved by further research now taking place.

Spring and early summer are peak risk times for suicide in Ireland as elsewhere. The reason for this seasonal rhythm is not clear but the same phenomenon is seen in the fluctuating incidence of depressive illness (which carries the highest risk of suicide). The peaking of suicide and of depression in spring and early summer may have something to do with as yet poorly understood alterations in the biological rhythms of body chemistry.

Ireland is somewhat unusual in that our suicide rates are higher in rural than in city areas. In most industrialised countries the reverse is the case. Whatever the benefits of country living for healthy people with a good family life, the availability of open water, poisons and shotguns make the Irish countryside a dangerous place for the isolated depressive.

Modern medical studies of suicide usually find evidence of severe depression preceding the act. Psychological autopsy often reveals that depressive illness has gone untreated even though the depressed person has sought professional help. The medical profession is now showing great concern to improve expertise in the detection and treatment of depression, and medical schools emphasise the skills needed to diagnose this condition and to assess suicide risk.

The story of suicide is not told without reference to the current, global epidemic of non-fatal deliberate self-poisoning by prescribed drugs, sometimes called attempted suicide or parasuicide. The invention of safe sleeping pills in the 1950s presented the community for the very first time with a relatively painless way of opting out for a while from the troubles of life. For some years now deliberate self-poisoning has been the second commonest cause of admission to British general hospitals and it is not uncommon in this country. At first, self-poisoners were seen as failed suicides, but the psychiatrist Erwin Stengel who carefully interviewed hundreds of parasuicide survivors, has shown clearly that they are different in many important respects from failed suicides. Parasuicides, for example, are younger, more often women and have no clear-cut intention to die, although some miscalculate the odds, such as Marilyn Monroe, and a substantial minority finally dies by suicide. There seems to be a muddled motivation amounting to a wish to sleep. The act may follow a difficult, inter-personal crisis and is often facilitated by alcohol: one English survey recently showed that St Valentine's Day is a peak risk period. The principal motivation is seen as a cry for help; a cry often ignored by a public which disapproves of and is frightened by this kind of behaviour. There may be twenty to forty times more cases of parasuicide than of suicide or failed suicide. Figures are hard to come by because only a minority of parasuicides comes to medical notice at emergency departments. The dangers of overdosage are exacerbated by the great increase in prescribing in recent times and also because several antidepressive drugs are dangerous if the prescribed dose is exceeded.

The latest chapter in the story of suicide is still being written. It has always puzzled psychiatrists that only a small minority of mentally ill persons, even those at greatest risk, actually take their own lives. Very recently it has been found that the brains of suicide victims are depleted of an important chemical messenger. This substance, called serotonin, is one of the most important neurotransmitters in the nervous system. It has for some time been suspected that lack of serotonin is one of the main reasons behind the development of severe depressive illness with its attendant risk of suicide. This suspicion has been strengthened by the finding that successful treatment restores the supplies of serotonin to the brain. Consequently, there is currently some excitement in medical circles at the future prospect of being able to identify would-be suicides in advance, so that effective treatment may be instituted in time.

Thus, our attitudes over 2,000 years have turned full circle. From a crime against the State, then a crime against God, then society's crime against the person, we come to the twentieth-century notion of suicide as a public health problem and finally to serotonin. *From sin to serotonin.* From 'self-murder in the 180th degree' to a regrettable but safe and sterile medical statistic. This abdication of responsibility by the body politic, however, fails to convince. The Utopian caring society where suicide is not needed is as far away as ever, not least because the citizens of Sir Thomas More's Utopia were allowed to commit suicide when life becomes unbearable.

Although this country still ranks as one of the lowest suicide countries in the world, it would be naive to expect that we can withstand indefinitely the worldwide trend towards secularisation, the break-up of the nuclear family and the abandonment of traditional values, factors which are increasingly cited as prime causes for rising suicide rates, especially amongst the young. It is certain that medical scientists alone cannot solve the problem. Ironically, and paradoxically, what seems to be needed now is a return to basic Christian virtues. If the sanctity of life is really worth all we say it is then surely the life of the would-be suicide is worth saving? Here, the example of the Samaritan organisation shows the way in the provision of emergency telephone helpline services for the lonely, the despairing and the suicidal. A recent sympathetic pastoral letter suggests that the Church is ahead of legislators in sensing the need for reform.

A necessary prelude to any anti-suicide programme will have to be an honest appraisal of the extent of the problem. This will need much more research which may in turn lead to new legislation to de-criminalise an act which, after all, cannot be punished in this life and for which innocent family survivors should not be expected to suffer. To fail to do this now that the cat is out of the bag will be to confirm that pagan fears of the suicide's ghost still linger on in the minds of Irish people. True, we no longer bury the corpse with a stake through the heart, but then this may only be because we think someone else will solve the problem. But suicide is everyone's business. It has added itself to previously taboo subjects such as child abuse, drug addiction and the AIDS virus, all of which, just like suicide, are acknowledged symptoms of social 'dis-ease'.

So what of the future? Suicide is a fact of death and we all must live with it. It will only lose its sting when we lose our fear of death, and that is not in prospect. Suicide is nothing if it is not a tragedy. It is *not* a scandal. It is scandalous only to regard it so. We should not, of course, encourage suicide but it must be de-criminalised. Until this is done, we cannot overcome the stigma conferred on families. There is no evidence that de-criminalisation stimulates more suicide. On the contrary, it has long been known to psychiatrists that it is a relief to the suicidal to know they are not alone (and that extreme despair is at most a transitory emotion). And is there not something unacceptable about an archaic law which serves no purpose and which is merely a relic of an age when the State used weapons of taboo and magic to control not only the lives but also the deaths of ordinary people?

Merely to de-criminalise suicide, whilst it is unlikely to stimulate more suicides, could have unwelcome side-effects if it means reverting to coroners' verdicts as the sole basis for national suicide statistics. In other countries it is well established that the more legalistic the approach to defining suicide, the fewer the cases which are found and the more which are concealed behind open verdicts and amongst those coded 'undetermined'. There would be great advantages to retaining a dual system of reporting mortality statistics such as that employed in Switzerland, where the attending doctor fills out two certificates, one for burial purposes only (which does not mention suicide) and the other which is anonymous and confidential and which includes suicide amongst a long list of modes and causes of death. In this way, the Swiss claim to have good suicide statistics while preserving confidentiality and the privacy of the family.

And what of public attitudes to suicide? Traditional kinship values which might protect against suicide cannot be recreated overnight, but at least we can recognise that depression is a morbid and dangerous state that is susceptible not only to medical help but also to simple neighbourly support. No psychiatric service can be without the capacity to provide expert counselling to suicidally bereaved families. For the mythical Greek hero, Sisyphus, who was condemned to perpetually push his rock up the hill only to see it roll down again, life was still worth living although manifestly absurd. In the words of Albert Camus, 'his rock was his thing', that is, life itself is what makes living worthwhile. For now, those of us who can must support others who doubt this, and throw our weight in on the side of life. Sigmund Freud in a rare burst of optimism provided a parable of hope for our day when he observed that 'life loses in interest when the highest stake in the game, life itself, may not be risked. People really die and not one by one but in their tens of thousands every single day. Life has, indeed, become interesting again.'

THREE

Schizophrenia: the myth and the reality

Dermot Walsh

Schizophrenia is a word which has become popular in English usage. Its most common application in ordinary parlance appears to be derogatory and implies a basic conflict between two lines of thought or of action. This usage is often resented by those with the most personal experiences of the disease — experiences that are too often painful. In fact, schizophrenia is a major psychiatric disorder arising predominantly in young people, sometimes lasting a lifetime and often extremely destructive of an individual's capacity to live and function in a useful and productive fashion.

The primary disturbance of schizophrenia is that of the capacity to think clearly, without interruption and logically in a problem-solving sequence. It is difficult for people outside psychiatry to understand how mystifying and disturbing this problem can be. To have your thinking process so derailed that you cannot think clearly because your thoughts no longer progress in an orderly fashion is to have something strike at the very roots of your humanity. Baffled, one logically seeks explanation and, since none is forthcoming, attributes these deroutements of thought to external factors. One believes, in short, that some outside agency is interfering with them.

Sometimes, subjective control over one's own thinking processes will become so lost that irrelevant subject matter intrudes on the main stream of thought and disrupts it; again the sufferer is likely to blame alien forces. Because thought is so fundamental to all that we do, the thought disruption of schizophrenia renders us unable to concentrate, work out and solve problems. Also, because the product of thought — namely, speech — is the mechanism by which we relate to others, the sufferer is debarred from communicating with his fellow human beings.

Because of the thought disturbance they are experiencing, those who suffer from schizophrenia often identify the external world and those in it as hostile towards them. From this grow the mistaken beliefs, called delusions, which are so common in the illness. Sometimes too, for reasons that are imperfectly understood, persons suffering from schizophrenia may hear voices talking aloud to them and these are referred to as hallucinations.

The resulting look of puzzlement and bafflement, difficulty in communication and solitariness create an image of strangeness, bizarreness, in those who suffer from schizophrenia. It is this which, uncomprehendingly, has led the public to create a stereotype of madness without understanding in any way the nature of the underlying process and the suffering that it is causing.

Because of the serious and corrosive nature of their illness, their incapacity to think clearly, to concentrate, to work out solutions to problems and to relate to fellow human beings, schizophrenics are often condemned to a life apart, isolated from gainful employment, from marriage, from friendship and so on. They are therefore prone to become marginalised, living on the fringes of society, sometimes homeless, unable to benefit from what society has to offer and hampered from contributing towards it.

So far, I have concentrated on the symptoms of schizophrenia and the effects these have on the sufferer. I will deal later with the more scientific aspects of the disease, particularly those relating to cause and treatment. But before doing so, I wish to examine the early perceptions of schizophrenia and madness throughout history, from the early Greeks and Celts to the present day.

There is ample documentary evidence from early civilisations that 'madness' has always existed. The Greeks, for example, were not alone involved in identifying mental aberrations, but also in classifying them. Thus it was they who first identified melancholia or what we would call depression today. They also identified hysteria. The Druids were also believed to have been capable of producing insanity; and, in the pagan ages and often far into Christian times, madness is believed to have been brought on by a malignant magical agency, usually the work of some devil. For that purpose, the Druid preferred a 'madman's wisp' or a 'fluttering wisp' — that is, a little wisp of straw or grass — into which he pronounced some horrible incantation. Then, watching his opportunity, he flung it into the face of his victim who at once became insane.

These early notions of the capacity of authoritarian figures to produce madness are repeated in the *Annals of the Four Masters* for the year 986. Often the Druids could malign a whole army so that soldiers were enervated and overwhelmed in battle. Much more recently, Lady Wilde noted that when a sheaf of corn, after its dedication to Satan and a malediction pronounced against the enemy, was buried in the ground and allowed to rot, then would the person so accursed wither away and die. These examples seem to indicate that there existed in Ireland up until fairly recently the equivalent of the phenomenon of voodoo death described in other cultures.

When it came to looking after the insane, it was also held in the old Gaelic culture that madness was particularly common in, and people were banished to, a place called *Gleann na Gealt*. Also, earlier culture was not particularly kind when it came to looking after its mad. Stories exist, for which there is good legendary support, of such treatments as burying the insane in holes in the ground up to their necks.

Later on, from the medieval era, descriptions of individuals, though not common, have been given that satisfy most observers as fulfilling the criteria of what we today would call schizophrenia. Later still, in the mid-eighteenth century, the growth of private madhouses became a common phenomenon. This was boosted by the Victorian policy that all madness should be confined in asylums both for the good of the lunatic and for society as a whole. As a result, further accommodation was provided, and by 1900 half a per cent of the Irish population was to be found in psychiatric hospitals.

The increase in the proportion of those hospitalised in asylums — or district mental hospitals as they were later to become — continued throughout the twentieth century. By 1958, 21,000 (or put another way 0.7 per cent of the population of the 26 Counties) were to be found in district mental hospitals. This was almost double the rate of mental hospitalisation apparent in our neighbouring western European countries.

By far the greater proportion of people who resided in psychiatric hospitals were suffering from schizophrenia. It was therefore believed for a long time that schizophrenia was a more common disorder here than elsewhere. But this merely reflects a greater capacity for recourse to hospital care than elsewhere rather than any greater incidence or prevalence of the disorder in Ireland.

Some studies were undertaken in the 1950s and 1960s which are worth referring to. For example, it was at one time claimed by American researchers that Irish schizophrenics had shown characteristic symptoms in schizophrenia which were different from those symptoms shown by schizophrenics of other nationalities. Indeed, one celebrated researcher claimed that 'the English are calmer than the Irish when schizophrenic'. Other observers spoke about the Hibernian psychosis and up to twenty or thirty years ago it was common to hear psychiatrists in Ireland talk about the 'Western seaboard psychosis'. This indicated a particular pattern of quiet withdrawal with the concomitant destruction of capacity to relate emotionally. This, it was said, was more common among Irish patients than else-where, and in Ireland it was said to be particularly more common in patients from the West.

A further study of hospitalised schizophrenics compared those who were Irish born with those American born and concluded that male Irish patients as compared to the Americans showed widespread fear of and hostility towards female figures. They consequently exhibited predominantly confused sexual identification, consisting for the most part of repressed and latent homosexual tendencies. Research also claimed to show that Irish patients did not, in general, act out their emotional difficulties by contrast with an Italian-born group. On the other hand, they showed the same amount of disturbed outwardly directed behaviour as the Italians. The study concluded that the Irish patients tended to retreat into fantasy and develop paranoid delusions which often consisted of hostility towards female figures. Furthermore, in the Irish, there was often a sig-nificantly greater degree of preoccupation with guilt and sin. Not surprisingly — as this is an old chestnut not borne out by more modern research — abuse of alcohol was deemed to be more common in the Irish schizophrenic.

Another more recent and often cited work by a prominent US anthropologist attempting to relate high mental hospitalisation rates (identifying these with high mental illness rates) to rural poverty at a time when Ireland had never been more prosperous, illustrates the foolhardiness of building elaborate explanatory hypotheses on inaccurate data. While some of these findings may have had some basis in reality a quarter of a century or more ago, it is doubtful if this is the case today. Anyway, there are serious scientific difficulties with studies of the kind from which these findings derive. For example, they are not 'blind' to the racial identity of the individual, nor can they by their nature be so. This indicates that the raters will be biased in favour of the hypothesis which they are testing. In short, the validity of the studies can be seriously questioned.

Now to the causes of schizophrenia, a disease which, incidentally, affects approximately one per cent of human populations. There was a time in medical history when diseases of a simple kind such as cholera, dysentry and so on were still rife. Such conditions were simple in disease terms as they were caused by a single agent. This was a bacterium, which made its effects felt very shortly after invading the human organism and which could be recovered from the human body itself. All of these diseases have now been conquered by medical science or by improved living conditions. Not so with cardiovascular disease, cancer and major mental disorder. These latter diseases are very complex in that they are caused not by one single factor but by a great matrix of agents. These agents may be infectious, toxic, genetic, or whatever, working together in a highly complex fashion over many years before the end-product of malign interaction — that is, the disease itself — appears.

For all these diseases there is no simple causative explanation and this is equally true of schizophrenia. We know in the case of schizophrenia that some families are more prone to the disease than others. At the same time, we know that the majority of cases of schizophrenia occur in families which have no history of it. Studies on twins — and more recently on the children of schizophrenic parents adopted by non-schizophrenic parents — suggest that hereditary factors are important in some cases. Nevertheless, hereditary or genetic factors of themselves are not sufficient to cause the disorder. Therefore it is necessary to look to environmental or external factors (whether these be of a physical or social nature) which must interact with the genetic factors (whatever they may be) to cause the disorder in a particular individual.

It is likely that both these adverse environmental and genetic factors predispose the brain to interference with those processes and connections within the brain which govern thought. What precise brain chemicals are involved is the subject of continuing study. Some help is being given by our knowledge that in some cases of schizophrenia certain drugs can be effective in controlling some of the symptoms of the disorder.

Furthermore, newer technologies that have been developed in the field of physical medicine have increased our capacity to investigate genetic influences and also to elucidate brain damage and brain function. All of these are being used intensively now in the study of schizophrenia and already some promising leads have begun to emerge. But it would be naive to represent that knowledge of the 'cause' and the 'cure' for schizophrenia are around the corner. They may take much longer to find. Indeed, it is not even clear that we are dealing with a single disorder: it may be that the clinical entity which we call schizophrenia is the final common pathway of any number of different and highly complex disease processes.

As to the treatment of schizophrenia, there are currently two main approaches. The first is the application of drugs that are believed to counteract a substance in the brain called 'dopamine'. This is suspected of having something to do with the schizophrenic process on empirical grounds. The second treatment approach is the provision of suitable alternatives to institutional care so that the disease does not progress. These alternatives should also ensure that the further impairments of institutionalisation — which undoubtedly hampered recovery in years gone by — do not occur.

There is, in addition, a school of thought which believes that the outcome for individual schizophrenic patients is considerably improved when there is an understanding and supportive attitude on the part of relatives. Already there is some experimental evidence to suggest that intensive working with families of schizophrenic persons substantially improves the outcome for individual patients and reduces the progression of the condition.

As mentioned earlier, schizophrenia affects approximately one per cent of human beings and the outcome for the majority of these is not too unsatisfactory. However, there is a small number of affected patients for whom the outcome is relatively poor. Because schizophrenia is a disease of early life — usually beginning in the late teens or early twenties — the prospects of a lifelong impairment is serious from their point of view and from the point of view of their families. It is also serious from a public health perspective, leading as it does to considerable impairment over decades and with the involvement of almost continuous patient care at not inconsiderable expense.

However, these rather gloomy thoughts should be dispelled by recalling that, compared with the past, schizophrenia research has attracted far better calibre researchers, is better funded and, because of technical advances in many areas of science, is much more amenable to investigation than was formerly the case. Unfortunately, it is still a poorly funded research area when compared to heart disease and cancer with which it vies as a major public health problem of our time.

Much of what has been written in the earlier parts of this paper relates to the institutional care of mental illness. Indeed, a good deal of the stereotyping that has emerged in relation to psychiatric illness is more the result of this process than of mental illness itself. It is now known that the process of institutionalisation, once the acute symptoms of schizophrenia have passed, is responsible for most of the subsequent impairments and disabilities in patients. That they are not the consequence of the illness itself is increasingly being realised.

Indeed, there is much evidence to show that the worst effects of schizophrenia are apparent in the earlier years of the illness and that once these have passed the symptoms tend to recede, provided that people are not chronically institutionalised. It is for this reason that the process of de-institutionalisation — or non-institutionalisation in the first place — has been growing throughout mental health services worldwide. This is also the trend in Ireland. For example, during the 1960s, 1970s and 1980s there has been a continuous decline in the numbers hospitalised. These now stand at approximately 10,000, or less than half the 1958 figure. The continued provision of community alternatives to hospitalisation has stood the Victorian policy of institutionalisation on its head and has continued to reduce inpatient numbers. They will continue to fall, we believe, until hospital rates have fallen to somewhere between 0.5 and one per thousand of population from the current rate of 3.5.

This is not to say that some schizophrenic patients do not require continuing care but rather that this is best provided outside the traditional psychiatric hospital. Accordingly, alternatives which on aggregate are described as 'community care' are being provided. These include day hospitals, day centres, community residences and an extensive network of support provided by professional people such as nurses, doctors, social workers and so on. These will work more closely with patients in their own homes and in primary medical care, that is, care provided by general practitioners.

Community care appears to cause as much emotional response as lunacy itself did in the old days. One might say that one form of prejudice has replaced another. Generally, there is a feeling that the uncomfortable nature of mental illness to those not mentally ill poses a threat to all of us, no doubt explaining such reactions. This is not to say that poorly organised community care is not to be deprecated. A growing number of homeless in very large urban settings — some of whom are undoubtedly mentally ill and some of whom are de-institutionalised patients — should remind us that quality assurance should be uppermost in the minds of those directing community care programmes.

So far in Ireland much has been done in many parts of the country towards getting away from the unacceptable conditions which have prevailed in some large psychiatric hospitals in the past. They are being replaced by a more humane and better quality community care service. The government, through the Department of Health, is committed to moving towards community care and away from large psychiatric hospitals, some of which have already become largely redundant. This philosophy is enshrined in a recent policy document on the future of the mental health services in Ireland, called *Planning for the Future*. There is, as I have already said, substantial evidence now that this philosophy of short-term hospital care followed by community support is infinitely better for all concerned: for the staff, some of whom have themselves become institutionalised, and for the sufferers from schizophrenia and from other mental illnesses.

FOUR

The Child and the Family

Michael Fitzgerald

Our forebears showed great foresight when they put forward the sentiment in the 1916 Proclamation about 'cherishing all the children of the nation equally'. The democratic programme of the first Dáil in 1919 was equally on the mark when it stated that 'It shall be the first duty of the Republic to make provision for the physical, mental and spiritual wellbeing of the children.' They were noble aspirations. Yet today we have an extremely unequal society as far as children are concerned. This is particularly true in disadvantaged urban areas where there are considerable numbers of children with behaviour problems. They feel that life is not worth living, they show evidence of poor school progress and of being victims of abuse both inside and outside the family. As Yeats said, 'Things fall apart, the centre cannot hold.' It is a phrase with great meaning when describing these tragic children whose worlds have fallen apart. They show persistent behaviour disturbances, including childhood anxiety and depression.

It is sad but accurate to report that child deprivation is nothing new. It has existed through the centuries. In the 1700s and 1800s thousands of unwanted infants were sent to the Dublin Foundling Hospital. Many of them died there. In the first seven years of the hospital's existence 4,000 children were admitted and more than 3,000 died. The hospital used to give £2 per year to women who were willing to nurse these infants, and there are several reports of infants being murdered after the women received the money. The bodies were found in graves with the hospital brand still on them. Such horrific incidents may not happen today, but the results of contemporary research are still highly disturbing.

For ten years I have studied psychological problems in children and adolescents in modern-day Ireland. Many of my studies focussed on disadvantaged areas and distressing results were found. For any of us zest for life is fundamental. Yet when we asked nine- to eleven-year-olds if they felt life was worth living, 15 per cent thought that it was not most of the time, while a further 18 per cent thought it wasn't worth living sometimes.

In studying female adolescents, 15 per cent showed evidence of significant psychological stress — this in a normal inner city school. Eleven per cent admitted to often crying; 7 per cent to often thinking about killing themselves; 10 per cent to often being unhappy, sad or depressed and 6 per cent said they often used alcohol or drugs.

In a normal pre-school we found that 16 per cent of the children in a disadvantaged area were showing evidence of behaviour problems. The figures were higher in primary school. Eighteen per cent of ten and eleven year-old boys were showing evidence of formal psychiatric disorder. The rates were higher still in the families of the unemployed. When we compared urban and rural schools we found that urban schools had over twice as many children with behaviour problems as their rural counterparts.

These studies reveal quite clearly the results of disadvantage. Children suffer the consequences of financial strain, marital problems, parental mental illness, less good schools. They live in a community where learned helplessness pervades. Such disadvantaged groups have a low sense of control over the forces that impact on their lives. Our research has shown that some of the parents have significantly higher levels of hopelessness than parents in the community generally.

It is clear that almost everything that impacts on parents will also impact on children. This happens in many different ways. If parents are spending considerable time dealing with financial arrears and rent, electricity bills and mortgages, they will have less time left for their children. Research by the Combat Poverty Agency shows that in dealing with moneylenders, 8 per cent of parents said that they took the stress out on their children, while 13 per cent said the children had to go without, because of moneylending.

Poverty and debt increase the social isolation of families. Children do not have money to go on holidays, attend music classes or generally engage in extra-curricular activities. All of these would boost their self-esteem. Mothers have to carry a disproportionate burden of the stress related to poverty which they experience as a sense of shame, guilt, embarrassment and powerlessness. They have a sense of feeling excluded and having to suffer the unsympathetic comments from privileged groups. All of this increases the psychological stress on the mother. Indeed, some of our Irish studies have shown that over a quarter of these mothers show significant symptoms of anxiety or depression. The result is that poverty and disadvantage undermine parenting ability. Ultimately, this can lead to a higher rate of child behaviour problems.

So far I have concentrated on the role of social and economic deprivation in explaining child behaviour problems. But the issue is more complicated. Nietzsche might well say it is not surprising that children are disturbed at this time in history. They are, as he put it, 'children of a fragmented, pluralistic, sick and weird period'. But there are many more associations to explore.

The first issue to be considered is that of genetics. Indeed, there is an Irish saying, '*treise duchas na Oiliunt*' (heredity is stronger than rearing). While this is a sweeping statement, there is some truth in it in relation to certain disturbed children. For a start, there is evidence for a genetic component in a condition called childhood autism.

This condition has, as its core feature, relationship difficulties. There is also a weak genetic component in a subgroup of children with conduct and delinquent problems which persist into adult life. Finally, genetic mechanisms may also play a part in the connection between social oddities in childhood and schizophrenic psychoses in adult life.

A second major issue came to prominence in the 1950s when John Bowlby claimed that maternal deprivation in infancy led to permanent damage to children. The issue proved to be much more complex. Subsequent research showed that the positive and negative experiences throughout childhood, adolescence and later life would have a considerable effect on the development of the person. The Bowlby theory had to be revised. It was pointed out in 1985 that markedly adverse experiences in infancy carried few risks for later development if the subsequent rearing environment was a good one. What is more, it was established that daycare children tended to be less apprehensive of new situations, were more peer oriented and more assertive. There was also no evidence of greater likelihood of psychiatric disorder. In the case of Bowlby and his thesis of maternal deprivation, the lesson is: beware of experts!

Some further issues in explaining child behaviour problems have been explored in a series of Irish studies. Firstly, in controlled studies we have shown significantly increased levels of marital disharmony in parents of disturbed children. It would appear that marital disharmony leads to poor supervision of children and to erratic parenting. It also creates a model of family discord based on aggression, inconsistency and hostility.

In another study we examined children of mothers who had been admitted to hospital as psychiatric patients. Over 50 per cent of their children showed evidence of social incompetence. It is possible that parental mental illness undermines a parent's ability, emotionally, to deal with their children's needs. It can impair the parent's ability to model appropriate social behaviour for them. Interestingly, there is evidence that boys are more at risk than girls from the effects of parental mental illness.

Finally, when we studied the home environments of children, we found that families that had low levels of warmth, affection and acceptance had significantly higher rates of children with behaviour problems.

Looking at the Irish context, however, it is imperative to return to the issue of poverty and disadvantage. It is prevalent in a society such as ours with its class divisions. There is an Irish saying:

> *An te ata Thuas oltar deoch air*
> *An te ata Thios bualtear cos air*

which translates as 'the top dog's health is always drunk, there are only kicks for the underdog'. This saying identifies the two orbits within which children live out their lives. These orbits are more distinct in urban areas. On the one hand there is the advantaged orbit, where children come from privileged circumstances, have good pre-school and school education and get good jobs, all of which bolsters their mental health. They marry successfully, parent their children successfully and their children continue in this orbit. The advantages are obvious. Eithne Fitzgerald has shown how a child from Foxrock is eighty times more likely to reach third-level education than a child from a disadvantaged area of Dublin.

Of course, affluence can create its own problems. Abundance of money can lead to too rapid gratification of a child's needs. This can result in a lack of motivation, boredom and a lack of clear identity. Apart from such extremes, however, it would appear that the children of the middle class are least at risk within the orbit they inhabit: no disadvantage, no excess either. Nevertheless, we know that in each class in a middle-class school there is a small number of disturbed children. These children tend to come from homes with family and marital conflict and/ or serious parental mental illness.

The alternative orbit is the disadvantaged one. Children live in disadvantaged circumstances in the presence of considerable marital disharmony, parental mental illness, financial strain and the sense of helplessness and lack of hope. Such less well-off groups have earlier parenthood, larger families, lower usage of health clinics, are slower to seek medical advice and are less responsive to health education campaigns. The hidden costs of health have a much greater impact on these families. There is the time and effort required of parents to get health care for their children when there is no telephone and wages have to be lost to bring children to a health centre. In McGee and Fitzgerald's study of children hospitalised for gastroen- teritis, they found that 33 per cent of mothers had difficulty in organising the finance to visit their children. Only 36 per cent had access to a family car. It was also of interest that the mothers of children most likely to be hospitalised for gastroenteritis were the least likely to have the resources, or access to facilities, to visit the hospital.

The highly influential Black Report published in Britain in 1980 is equally relevant to the Irish situation and is worth quoting. The first point is that children born to unskilled workers are four times more likely to die in the first year of life than those born into professional families. The second point is that boys in these families are twice as likely to die between the ages of one and fourteen, while girls are one and a half times more likely to die. The third point is that the children of professionals have a five year longer life expectancy. Clearly, all of these factors show the huge effect of disadvantage on children.

There is, perhaps, no more controversial an issue than that of how to tackle disadvantage, how to foster health and flourishing home environments for the children. It is far more complicated than simply being an issue of money. Garret FitzGerald has pointed out that Gross Domestic

Product per head of population is 35 to 40 per cent lower in Ireland than in our near neighbours. While the basic rates of social welfare are relatively high, by comparison, and our politicians can take some credit for this, it should not deflect us from the attraction of a basic income system.

One obvious problem which needs to be tackled is the placement of families from disadvantaged areas in housing long distances from their family roots and friends. This has led to a negative psychological impact. When we compared Irish mothers with mothers living in Malaysia, we found a far lower rate of anxiety and depression in Malaysian mothers. This was most likely explained by their circumstances: they lived with their extended families and therefore had far more social linkage and support. The need to reduce such forms of isolation in Ireland is critical. There is a role for the whole community, including neighbours and clergy, in tackling this issue. Some of the Irish families, although in good-quality housing from a structural point of view, nevertheless feel alienated because they are so far from their friends and grandparents. They are effectively, psychologically, homeless. This problem has been complicated in recent years by the well-intentioned £5,000 surrender grant for tenants in local authority housing. This has led to families moving out of their areas. When those who move are those with leadership qualities the overall community competence is reduced.

A further complicating factor which needs to be examined is the segregation of public and private housing. It is my belief that from a psychological perspective we might have some less stressed families if there was adequate mixing. This would have the effect of raising the general level of community competence and support. It could also improve the social mobility of disadvantaged groups who are marginalised and isolated in ghettoised housing estates. A policy of mixing accommodation could also have the effect of reducing the suspicion between classes. It certainly would have the effect of boosting the esteem of some disadvantaged children; suddenly they would see that they could compete successfully with their more advantaged counterparts. In short, it is my experience that the private value of the middle class, with their separate housing, may not be in the public good, nor, especially, in the interests of the disadvantaged child.

One can hardly talk about children without discussing schools and their impact. It has been shown that less effective schools are twice as likely to show evidence of poor school attendance and to have children who leave school without scholastic qualifications. In contrast, even when children are reared in institutions, when they have positive school experiences they are three times as likely to plan their choice of career and marriage partner. So what can schools do in the preventative area?

For a start, at pre-school level, there is evidence that programmes which allow children to plan their environment help them to actively learn. A study has revealed that when children from such programmes were followed up at twenty-one years of age there were significant gains between disadvantaged children who had such programmes and those who had not. The gains included more of the students completing secondary school and going on to third-level education. Fewer of them were arrested and significantly fewer were on social welfare. These studies were undertaken in the US where it was shown that the programme was cost effective. There was a four-dollar return on every dollar invested in the community. There were reduced demands on the community in terms of special education or costs to the legal authorities. Such schemes can obviously work and they show the value of preventative interventions at pre-school level.

Moving on to the primary level, Professor Kolvin has shown that direct intervention at this stage works. Group therapy for children showing evidence of behavioural problems is effective in reducing them. Again, such direct intervention programmes should be pursued. However, we are limited sadly by society's emphasis on treating illness rather than on prevention: over half of the health budget goes into the general hospital programme. It is a policy in need of reassessment and change.

At secondary school there is now much anecdotal evidence that a highly academic curriculum is not appropriate to weaker students. In this context the need for remedial care is of paramount importance. I would also suggest, however, that alterations being made to the curriculum emphasising the development of planning skills will help children plan for their future lives. That this will be productive is evidenced from studies among adolescents. These have shown that those with an ability to plan their lives were at much less risk of making unsatisfactory marriages and experiencing marital breakdown as adults.

Another area where weaker students could be helped would be in the development of social skills. It is also likely that various vocational skills, such as those covered by the vocational preparation and training programme, would be of more interest to them. It would probably also increase school attendance. I would also suggest that because children from disadvantaged areas have so little chance of getting to third-level education, universities and colleges should consider outreach programmes. They should also set àside places for children from disadvantaged areas.

There would, of course, be costs attached to many of these measures. But the long-term benefits cannot be ignored. For example, there is an established link between education and usage of the health service, certainly in terms of the hospitalisation of children. It was shown in Israel that when parents had an extra year's secondary schooling, their children had less hospitalisation as infants. Put in simple terms, the moral is that we have to spend now to save later.

At this point the fundamental question of what is required for the healthy development of children must be examined. Firstly, if children are to develop healthily they need air and food as well as love and praise. From a psychological point of view, while love is not enough on its own it certainly goes a long way. Freud put it so well and so accurately: 'If a man has been his mother's undisputed darling, he retains throughout life the triumphant feeling, the confidence in success, which not seldom brings actual success with it.'

The second most critical need of a child is for praise. Unfortunately with the older generation in Ireland there was confusion between praise and spoiling. Consequently, very many Irish children have suffered from a lack of praise in childhood because of parental fears that if they were praised they would be spoiled. While there is no doubt that spoiling exists, it is much less frequent than people think.

The third need which children have is for boosts to their self-esteem. It is clear that those children with high self-esteem and self-confidence are more resilient in the face of problems. In various studies we have found that children with problems had low self-esteem. We also found that self-esteem at school was reduced in children with problems who attended normal school but not in similar children attending a special school. This was because in special settings children were performing on a level with their peers. They were also more likely to be in smaller groups and therefore getting more praise from their teachers. What is absolutely clear is that nothing succeeds like success. It is critical for parents and teachers to provide children with success experiences in so far as this is humanly possible.

What about the psychotherapeutic treatment of disturbed children, children whose worlds have fallen apart? The child psychiatrist aims to help the child put the parts back together again, to give the child an opportunity to develop a centre or identity for themselves. A central feature of disturbed children's problems is alienation. The child psychiatrist, through psychoanalytic psychotherapy, is trying to reduce this alienation. By forming a bond with the alienated child the psychiatrist helps the individual understand the stresses that have brought about their current situation. Ibsen says, 'Everything must be borne alone — despair, resistance and defeat'. The child psychiatrist attempts to make sure that this does not happen.

The facts facing all of us in our professional lives are daunting, but clear: namely, that disturbed children and adolescents are hurt children and adolescents. They often respond to this hurt by taking revenge on their families, school and society. What is more, society often responds to them by taking further revenge which only aggravates the matter. It is our function to help these children and adolescents come to terms with their past hurts; to help them love and be loved. Then they are no longer, to quote Arnold in describing Beckett's characters, 'tormented with what seems to be an arid desert like inability to love or be loved'. We are trying to help them to live fully and to trust again. Our main task is to form long-term relationships with them over many years, whether in child psychiatry clinics or in local clubs and activities. If such long-term bonds can be formed with these children they can be helped through many difficult periods in their lives without damaging themselves or society.

It would be all too easy to forget that there have been certain gains for the Irish child in the last fifty years. For example, there has been increased awareness of the rights of children. The abolition of corporal punishment was also extremely important. There is a growing understanding of the importance of caring for children in small groups rather than large institutions. Lastly, our growing awareness of the needs of children to be cared for in the family context has been demonstrated by the increasing number of foster placements each year.

However, for the 1990s there is urgent need for a new children's agenda. The list of priorities is long. We need to evaluate scientifically the effectiveness of all aspects of the health care system for children. We need to prioritise all aspects of preventative health strategies. In education, our junior schools in particular could benefit from speech therapists' advice on children who have delays in language or who have speech problems. We also need an inspectorate of pre-school, daycare centres and children's homes to monitor standards of care. In the area of criminality and justice, the 1908 Juvenile Justice Act needs to be updated, and the age of criminal responsibility needs to increase from its current level of seven to fifteen years of age. And, while the Eastern Health Board has well-developed psychiatric services, there are areas of the country where these require urgent development. It is critical that the Departments of Health, Education and Justice work together. Our ultimate objective has to be to make our society more child centred. We need to give all our children a sense of belonging, to cherish them, not just verbally but in reality. It will take more than constitutional rhetoric to achieve it.

FIVE

Sexuality and the Irish

Frank O'Donoghue

It is, perhaps, unwise to think in terms of national stereotypes, as it is a small step from this to racial or ethnic prejudice. However, sexual stereotypes do exist: for example, the Swedes are associated with 'free love', thereby creating the undeserved reputation of being rather promiscuous. The Italian male is perceived as being somewhat macho in his demeanour and not noted for his marital fidelity. Fortunately for him, he is not married to the Spanish female, whose paroxysms of jealousy know no bounds!

By comparison, the Irish are often perceived as a sexually inhibited, priest-ridden, matriarchal nation. It is a view asserting that we have more problems with sexuality than other nations, and where alcohol is frequently seen as a symptom of our difficulties in dealing with our sexual problems. More importantly, it is a view which sees the Church's moral teaching as the root of all evils of sexual repression, which, it is alleged, is rampant in Ireland. Unfortunately, while people are quick to level this accusation, they are not so quick to sift through the relevant research to substantiate their claims.

The link between religion and sexuality was examined at an early stage by the original sex therapists, Masters and Johnson. Their conclusion was that no one religious group was culpable. Rather, they found that it was the strictness or orthodoxy of religious views which was important. In his regard, strict Catholic families were just as likely to produce sexual dysfunction as strict Jewish, Presbyterian or Hindu families. Indeed, of the patients attending our Psycho-Sexual Clinic at St Patrick's Hospital, we have found that religious groups are represented in approximately the same proportions as exist in the general population. Obviously, the vast bulk of our patients are Catholic (90 per cent), but there are also Church of Ireland (3 per cent), Presbyterian and Methodist (.5 per cent), Jews (.6 per cent), Hindus (.2 per cent) and Buddhists (.1 per cent). And in my experience I have seen sexual difficulties arise far more frequently from repressive, puritanical parental attitudes than from any traumatic episodes with a priest, religious nun or brother. In other words, I feel that many of these attitudes are passed from generation to generation through parents rather than through any direct involvement by the Church.

The wider question, however, needs to be addressed namely, are we more sexually inhibited than other nations and do we have more sexual problems here than else where? I am afraid the answers to these questions are no readily available and will not be for some time. Of all th problems which take people to see their doctor, none i more embarrassing than sexual failure. To give an example the average length of time it takes for someone to presen to our clinic for treatment for a non-consummated marriag (that is, a marriage where no penetration has occurred) i 3.5 years. We have had one couple who presented for hel after twenty years of a non-consummated marriage. I als know from talking to patients that, despite diligent ques tioning from their general practitioner, they have deliberatel misled their GP into believing everything was in order i the sexual side of their marriage. So when I am asked d we have more sexual problems than other nations, I simp reply that I do not know. I do not know whether thos clinicians engaged in sexual therapy are seeing merely th tip of the iceberg or the whole iceberg. The studies just d not exist.

My own impression, having worked both in Ireland and in Canada, is that we have probably the same amount of sexual dysfunction per head of population as other countries. But what exactly is this figure likely to be? The major studies of neurotic illness in general practice suggest that from perhaps 15 per cent to 30 per cent of patients suffer from neurotic or psychosomatic disorder. Yet the areas of human unhappiness which are more difficult to define, especially psycho-sexual difficulties, have come into prominence only relatively recently. And, even theoretically, it is hard to conceive of precise community prevalence figures.

Part of the problem is that it is hard to devise accurate yardsticks for measuring psycho-sexual problems. For a start, the major dysfunctions, such as male erectile impotency or premature ejaculation or, on the other hand, female arousal problems or orgasmic dysfunction, are not 'all or none' phenomena, but rather form a spectrum of dysfunction from mild to severe. In that context, the definition of premature ejaculation as inability to satisfy the partner in 50 per cent of sexual contacts might be useful for research, but is otherwise clearly arbitrary.

It also seems possible that some degree, often transitory, of sexual dysfunction may occur with couples who would otherwise be classified as having no problems at all. For example, an American study in 1978 analysed one hundred predominantly white, well-educated and happily married couples, who replied to a detailed marital questionnaire. Over 80 per cent of the couples reported that their marital sexual relations were happy and satisfying, and nearly 90 per cent said they would marry the same person if they lived their lives over again. Despite these results 40 per cent of the men reported erectile or ejaculation dysfunction and 53 per cent of the women reported arousal or orgasmic dysfunction. Also, 50 per cent of the men and 77 per cent of the women reported what the authors define as 'difficulties', for example, lack interest, difficulty in relaxing, too little frequency and so on. Further analysis suggested that it was the overall relationship aspect of the marriage that determined how most couples perceive the quality of their sexual relationship.

Looking at these and other studies, if one were asked to make an educated guess at the prevalence of dysfunction, one would hazard at around 20 per cent of the general population. As sexual counselling is in its early stages, not just in Ireland but in other countries as well, it will be some time before we develop something like a central data bank, which would then enable us to determine whether we are in fact contacting that 20 per cent who need help.

Now to the problems with which couples come seeking help. In this context, it is clear that we are not a great deal different from other nations. The experience of our clinic is based on over a thousand patients who have been seen over an eleven year period. I have recently examined our clinic files and the results make for interesting reading.

For example, five areas of concern in females were identified. One-third of all females presented with vaginismus leading to non-consummation of marriage. This is a condition where there is painful spasm of vaginal muscles, which leads to an inability to consummate the marriage. Another one-third of females complained of low levels of sexual drive. The final one-third was made up of painful sexual intercourse and an inability to derive enjoyment from sexual activity, while a small number of patients presented with anxieties about homosexuality.

Turning to the males, there is a greater variety of conditions which can lead them to seek help. By far the most common complaint was erectile dysfunction, making up 46 per cent of all dysfunction in males. In a further 6 per cent, the erectile difficulty was so severe that the marriage was not able to be consummated, so that erectile difficulties of all kinds constituted just over half of dysfunctional males.

The next most frequent male complaint was ejaculatory dysfunction. This made up approximately 16 per cent of our male dysfunctional patients, and was closely followed by homosexual anxieties, again just short of 16 per cent. These would be males, some of whom were homosexual, but some of whom merely had anxieties that they may be homosexual, usually based on some erectile failure when with a girl. Eight per cent of our presenting males complained of low level of sexual drive. A further 6 per cent complained of premature ejaculation.

Surprisingly, we had males presenting whose main reason in coming to the clinic was inadequate knowledge of sexuality and its knock-on effects. Two per cent of all our sexually dysfunctional males presented in this fashion. This figure is much higher than that of the female, who seldom if ever presents with inadequate information or misinformation. In the case of males, one is tempted to speculate that the pressure to be seen as macho, sophisticated and knowledgeable in sexual matters manoeuvres them into a position where they are then afraid or ashamed or embarrassed to seek out proper sexual information.

We also see sexual deviants at our clinic. Fourteen per cent, or about one in seven of cases referred, will complain of a sexual deviancy, although how this is defined is a matter of some dispute. For example, sexual deviancy could be defined as a persistent preference for sexual behaviour that departs from prevailing social standards. Alternatively, it could be defined as a persistent departure from genital intercourse with a single partner of approximately the same age and opposite sex, and this, of course, homosexuals would find offensive. Finally, there is the definition which says that sexual deviation is a degree of idiosyncrasy that is symptomatic of something, that is causing interference with function or that is socially intolerable or dangerous and accordingly calls for intervention.

Again, as with sexual dysfunction, the difficulties in establishing the prevalence of sexual deviation are practically insurmountable. As we have seen earlier, sexually dysfunctional couples, through embarrassment, are very reluctant to seek help. The same factors of embarrassment apply to the sexual deviant. However, outweighing that embarrassment is the simple fact that, in contrast to the sexually dysfunctional individual, the sexual deviant will find his behaviour enjoyable and simply may not wish to have treatment for it.

Indeed, many of our sexually deviant males will only present at the clinic somewhat reluctantly, either due to pressure from a spouse or because of disclosure of some illegal activity. It is generally agreed that, in treating psychological problems, motivation is important. It is doubly important in the treatment of sexually dysfunctional couples, as shown by the drop-out rate of anywhere between 25 per cent and 50 per cent. However, in the case of sexual deviants motivation is of paramount importance. And, not surprisingly, the angry, recalcitrant and disgruntled sexually deviant male who presents at our clinic purely to appease an angry spouse is very unlikely to co-operate with treatment or see it through to its conclusion.

A breakdown of the different types of sexual deviants who have presented is as follows:

(*a*) Almost one-third of all sexual deviants referred was made up of males accused of child molesting or paedophilia and males who to some degree interfered sexually with their own children. It must be pointed out that the majority of these referrals have come to our clinic in the last five or six years, with the increased media attention which is given to this behaviour generating many more referrals of late.

(*b*) The next most common group, numerically, were exhibitionists, who made up 14 per cent of all referrals. The notion that these are 'dirty old men' is erroneous contrary to the general public perception. In fact, the average age for indecent exposers was thirty.

(*c*) I am a little unhappy about including in the category of sexual deviant the condition known as trans-sexualism where individuals have the profound and unshakeable conviction that they are simply born with the wrong body, in other words, that they are basically a female personality trapped in a male body. Interestingly, we sometimes see the converse, that is, somebody that is firmly convinced that they should have a male body, even though they are to all intents and purposes female in external appearance. The reason for my discomfort with classifying these as deviants is that the majority of sexual deviants do what they do for the purpose of sexual gratification. The paedophiliac, the transvestite, the fetishist will all see sexual release as the end point of their behaviour. Not so the trans-sexual. Indeed, sexual gratification is low on their list of priorities. Nothing less than the reassurance of their new sex role will satisfy them, and in particular the acknowledgment from others of their new sex role is important to them. Nor are they insane; to the man in the street, the notion of gender reassignment surgery is an appalling idea, something he feels would only be wished for by somebody suffering from some form of madness. It is my experience that people who have had gender reassignment surgery, after careful selection, can lead contented and productive lives.

(*d*) Transvestites are superficially similar to trans-sexuals, and they made up 8 per cent of sexual deviants attending. These are people who again have a degree of disturbance of gender identity, but not to the extent of wishing gender reassignment surgery. In this regard they can be viewed as perhaps closer to sexual fetishists and these two groups together make up 18 per cent of our referrals. Transvestites can be graded into those who wear just the underclothing or those who wear the outer clothing as well and who move about publicly. The fetishist, on the other hand, will get sexual gratification simply from the close proximity of some inanimate object, which may or may not be an article of female clothing.

(*e*) Finally, there are the lesser known sexual deviancies. These will include voyeurism (which is the compulsion to observe the sexual activity of others), accounting for 7 per cent of our referrals; bestiality which makes up 5 per cent; and the thankfully rare conditions of masochism, sadism and necrophilia.

Returning to our national stereotypes, there is one well-known association that we cannot ignore in this paper, and that is the tendency for the Irish to abuse alcohol. Of those who presented at the clinic, 4 per cent already had a history of inpatient treatment for alcohol dependence, while a further 5 per cent were felt at assessment to have significant alcohol dependency.

I firmly believe that a significant percentage of alcoholics in this country begin their path to alcoholism by using alcohol to ease social anxieties. The Irish adolescent, in comparison to his Canadian counterpart, is distinctly less comfortable in heterosexual social situations. And, given a culture with its toleration for the man who likes a drink, it is no wonder that the young drinker quickly becomes dependent on the anxiety-relieving effects of alcohol.

Early in his career, alcohol will certainly improve his sexual functioning, at least in moderation. This is mainly because alcohol depresses or renders inoperative that part of our brain which puts the brakes on instincts such as the sexual or aggressive instincts. As a result, these instincts are given free rein, so that the individual would become somewhat more aggressive and certainly more flirtatious. This convinces the drinker that alcohol is good for him and gears him up for more easy social interaction.

However, with time, the depressing effects of alcohol take over. In its final stages, the alcoholic is too depressed to even attempt sexual relations. Combine this with the physical effects of alcohol on the liver, which will upset the hormonal balance of the person. Add on the effect on the nervous system, which will lead to peripheral neuritis and impotence and then consider the effects on the unfortunate partner who has to go to bed with this confused.

possibly aggressive, certainly depressed and intoxicated person. Overall, one can then see quite clearly the disastrous effects that excessive alcohol can have on the sex life of a partnership.

Before ending this paper, I feel it essential to make some attempt at international comparison of the extent of sexual disorder. There is clearly a lack of adequate data, yet we can make some comparisons in the type of patients who present to sex therapists looking for help. With this in mind, I looked back through our records over the years and compared them with those of a recently published study in the *British Journal of Psychiatry* by Catalan, Haughton and Day. Some differences between patients with sexual problems in the UK and in Ireland emerged if we look closely enough at the figures.

Taking females first, the most common complaint in the English study was of impaired sexual interest, representing 61 per cent of females presenting. The corresponding figure for Irish patients in our study was 30 per cent — and that is quite a discrepancy. So we should ask why do UK females complain in much greater percentages than the Irish patient. Perhaps it is an indication of a more assertive, less tolerant UK female, who, knowing that divorce is available, is not inhibited about asking for help in this area. In contrast, it may well be that the Irish couple may prefer to lapse into the familiar compromise of the silent, loveless marriage, where both the physical and emotional relationships have deteriorated beyond the point of no return.

Again, differences were encountered in the case of vaginismus, or spasm of the vaginal muscle. This appeared in 14 per cent of the UK sample, compared to the much higher 33 per cent here. Again, what can we tell? Clearly, a major factor here must be parental attitudes towards sexuality, purity and the issue of sex before marriage. Vaginismus is a rejection of penetration, an involuntary guarding of the entrance to the vagina, so that penetration is impossible. In a country where the phrase 'she had to get married' is used so frequently, it is surprising that we do not have an even higher incidence of vaginismus.

Finally, in relation to females, orgasmic dysfunction showed quite a discrepancy. The UK figure for this was 9 per cent, while again the Irish study yielded a much higher figure of 25 per cent. Again we could ask if this reflects the attitude that it is in some way sinful or unseemly to let go during sexual intercourse, something which is essential if complete sexual satisfaction is to be achieved.

Turning to comparisons between males, some interesting results again turned up. For example, problems with ejaculation comprised 6 per cent of the UK sample, but our figure was much higher at 16 per cent. Ejaculatory difficulties or retarded ejaculation may well stem from feelings of guilt, sexual inhibition and associated anxieties. It is also my experience in speaking to males at our clinic, that those who engage in pre-marital sex learn to suppress the sexual response in order to avoid pregnancy. Indeed, this form of contraceptive practice may also be seen in married couples as well.

Another interesting male result arose when comparing the results on premature ejaculation. In this case, the figures were considerably higher in the British study. In fact, some 16 per cent of those in Britain complained of the problem, while the figure here was much smaller at 7 per cent. So why should premature ejaculation present itself more frequently in the UK? There could be many reasons, but it is possible that the condition is simply not viewed as a problem by the Irish male. In other words, as long as his own sexual needs are met, it may not dawn on him that his problems in controlling sexual release may be having an adverse effect on the sexual functioning of his partner.

In comparing these figures, it is obvious that, while we have certain similarities with the British population, there are some very dramatic differences evident as well. They cannot be attributed to mere chance. But one can only speculate on their real significance. There are factors like our religious upbringing to account for; then there are our attitudes to marriage and divorce; and, of course, we cannot ignore how we perceive our sex in terms of dominance or submissiveness. But whatever the reasons, it is clear that there are many changes in our sexual attitudes taking place in recent decades, not to mention recent centuries. In concluding, I would like to refer briefly to these.

Firstly, we can look at our literature over the last few hundred years, which reflects some perceptible changes in our cultural attitudes and values. Indeed, we can see that we certainly have not been the sexually inhibited, prudish nation such as we have sometimes been portrayed. To begin with, we have Swift, the good Dean, remembered as much for his scatological verses as for his philanthropy. Later in the century Merriman's *Midnight Court* contains verses which would make the lyrics of the more raunchy pop songs of today sound positively demure. Then things changed in the 1800s, particularly with the influence of the Famine. Control, timekeeping, temperance, all began to creep into Irish society. In particular, the coming of the railways brought a sense of time, while Father Mathew and his Temperance Movement introduced control of appetites. This control became more entrenched during the latter part of the 1800s. It was not until the 1890s and the early 1900s that the work of Joyce opened the closet and placed on view the skeleton of sexuality. Later, Brinsley MacNamara took sexuality into a rural setting, and later still John McGahern and others continued the work, in the face of not just Church disapproval but also State censorship. More recently, the pendulum has begun to swing the other way, as a casual glance around the shelves of any bookstore or newsagent will now reveal.

It may be evident from our literature that a new liberalism has dawned in the area of Irish sexuality. However, it is more difficult to establish these changes scientifically. As

I said earlier, sex therapy is a relatively new discipline and we do not have enormous amounts of data to go on. Furthermore, because of its newness, the period over which we are trying to measure change is brief, unlike literature which spans the centuries. There is one observation which I feel, however, indicates that changes have occurred. This relates to people's willingness to come for help for sexual difficulties.

To try and measure this, I looked at the average duration of non-consummated marriages in 1979 as against those in 1989. The reason this particular condition was selected was that there are definite dates involved; we have the date on which the couple presented at our clinic. The result of my investigation was quite revealing. In 1979 the average duration of such a marriage was 5.5 years before presenting at our clinic. In 1989 the average duration had dropped to 2.8 years. It would seem from such a significant change that at least some shift in attitudes towards sexual problems has occurred, even over one decade.

It is an encouraging statistic with which to conclude this paper, indicating as it does a change whereby people are, at the very least, more prepared to present themselves for treatment of sexual dysfunction. At the very worst, it is a recognition by those with sexual problems that they need help. At best, it is a possible road to recovery for the individuals involved.

SIX

Dementia — the hidden disease

Margo Wrigley

Dementia is a frightening word which conjures up pictures of deranged elderly people running wild in a dangerous manner. Nothing could be further from the truth. It frightens mainly because it is such a poorly understood condition, despite the fact that approximately 20,000 Irish people currently suffer from it. That figure could be as high as 30,000, and the number will certainly rise significantly by the end of the century.

The literal meaning of dementia is 'loss of mind'. It occurs when certain disorders of the brain bring about a progressive loss of all the mind's functions. This leads to a deterioration in the person's ability to think, remember and concentrate and later to look after themselves. It usually starts silently and gradually gets worse over a couple of years before anyone notices something is wrong.

Dementia is a common condition among the elderly, with one in twenty of those over sixty-five being affected. This increases to one in five of those aged over eighty years; in other words, it becomes commoner with increasing age. Certainly, clinical experience indicates just how common it is. For example, a study carried out in Dublin in 1989, which examined all the elderly people in a quarter of the Eastern Health Board approved nursing homes, concluded that one half of the elderly residents were likely to suffer from dementia.

It is normal for a person to slow up gradually with increasing age and to take longer to learn new information such as names and addresses. However, it is not normal to lose the ability to use a cooker one has cooked on for many years. Such behaviour is more indicative of dementia than forgetfulness alone.

It may be months or years before anyone notices there is something wrong with the elderly person. Indeed, it is often only when looking back that relatives recognise that the problem has been present for some time. Hints may include being slower to catch on to things, forgetting new information quickly, not keeping the home as well as previously, nor, indeed, being as careful about personal hygiene and changing clothes.

In the beginning, only recent memory is affected. The result is that the person becomes disorientated as to time and unable to remember day-to-day or even minute-to-minute events. This interferes with the person's ability to manage their own life, for example, causing them to leave saucepans burning on the cooker. As the condition progresses, past memory also deteriorates. The sufferer may believe long-dead relatives are still alive. They may be unable to give the address of the house they have lived in for many years. With more severe deterioration in memory the sufferers may even be unaware of their own name. These problems are further exacerbated by difficulties with speech. Early signs are difficulties in naming objects. Later on, difficulties in understanding speech and expressing thoughts begin to appear. Sufferers also find it difficult to understand what is happening around them. This is particularly so at night when the darkness contributes to their confusion. At times like this, they may wake and insist on going to church. Poor memory in conjunction with poor grasp of their surrounding environments can lead to repetitive questioning. These factors can also lead to difficulty in making decisions which can cause problems with handling money and property.

As dementia progresses, sufferers lose the ability to carry out everyday tasks such as washing, dressing and housekeeping chores. Incontinence may also develop. Sleep problems are common, particularly wakefulness at night with a tendency to sleep during the day. Problems which may sometimes occur are behavioural or psychological symptoms and difficulties with mobility. The behaviour problems are restlessness, agitation, aggressiveness and uninhibited sexual behaviour; the psychological problems include mood disturbances such as anxiety and depression. These are more likely to occur in the early stages of the condition, especially if the sufferer realises all is not well with his memory. Other psychological problems could include odd ideas, such as elderly ladies with dementia accusing people of stealing their handbags. This occurs because they forget where they have left them. Occasionally, voices or visions are present, which are referred to as hallucinations.

The commonest cause of dementia is Alzheimer's disease which is wholly or partially responsible for three-quarters of all cases. Brain cells die prematurely, particularly in those parts of the brain involved in memory, reasoning and speech. Changes in brain structure and chemistry have been identified, but the cause of Alzheimer's remains unknown. Theories have abounded. Recently, aluminium in drinking water was implicated, but there is no convincing evidence for this. Unfortunately, Alzheimer's is an untreatable condition with average survival time following diagnosis normally seven years, although this can be very variable.

Multi infarct dementia is the second commonest form of dementia. It is caused by repeated small strokes damaging certain portions of the brain, resulting in the person developing the condition. This type of dementia is commonest in people with high blood pressure, in smokers and in those who have had strokes causing paralysis. Finally, about 5 per cent of dementia cases are due to a number of rare causes, some of which are treatable. The treatable causes are more likely to be found in younger people and in people with unusual symptoms. These symptoms should be more fully investigated with detailed tests such as brain scans.

Generally, dementia is seen in the elderly. However, it can develop in younger people, even those in their thirties and forties, when it is called pre-senile dementia. As you would expect, the commonest cause of this early onset of dementia is Alzheimer's disease. The occurrence of the symptoms is always a tragedy, but particularly so in younger people who may be in the middle of bringing up their families. Dementia may then mean the loss of the family breadwinner or of the mother who is no longer able to care for her children. Financial problems may be devastating if a salary is lost or money has to be found to pay for childcare.

As I mentioned earlier, dementia is a poorly understood condition in Ireland, with the result that it frightens many people. Families may view dementia as a disgrace, something to be ashamed of. Because of that, they do not talk about it and try to hide away their afflicted relative. Others not directly involved often respond by shying away from the problem, which results in those with dementia being stigmatised. Those living alone may be neglected until a crisis occurs which cannot be ignored.

Carers who look after relatives with dementia may receive little help until they reach breaking point. The response at such times of crises until recent years was to lock the demented away, often in large asylums far away from their families. As a society we showed our concern by turning a blind eye, following the principle, 'out of sight — out of mind'. The sufferer was doubly penalised for his affliction by being removed from his home, sometimes forcibly. Recently I had the pleasure of hearing an English psychiatrist talking on this issue. He neatly reversed the phrase 'out of sight — out of mind' to 'out of mind — out of sight'. It describes exactly what used to happen to those with dementia. The person loses his mind, in a manner of speaking, so he is removed to an institution where he is out of sight. By his absence, he no longer troubles society. Over the years it was gradually recognised that the so-called 'institutional' model of care — namely, locking the demented away — was not a humane way of caring for people. This was further enforced by a number of scandals involving institutions in the UK. As a consequence, a new model of care evolved, called the 'community' model of caring for those with dementia.

Specifically, community care has the underlying philosophy that sufferers of dementia should be maintained with dignity in their homes by providing appropriate services for them. This is based on the premise that most dementia sufferers prefer to stay in their own homes and that they function better when they are in familiar surroundings. This approach is most likely to succeed where there are family members who have the motivation and the strength to act as the backbone of care. Professional back-up is then provided to help families cope. The back-up should offer emotional support and information about the disease. The carers must also be offered regular breaks from the tasks of caring, a rapid response to crises and partnership in planning for the future needs of their relatives.

Community care is often said to be a cynical exploitation of the goodwill of carers. However, research has shown that many families would prefer to care for their disabled relatives but need practical and emotional support if they are to succeed. Such support is essential in the case of dementia which is acknowledged to be one of the most stressful illnesses in its effects on the carer. This is related not only to the amount of physical care the sufferer needs, but also to the grief of seeing a loved one slip away. Grief is prolonged and cannot be properly resolved until the sufferer dies.

In Ireland towards the end of 1988 a working party produced a report on caring for the elderly, including those suffering from dementia. The document was called

The Years Ahead — A Policy For The Elderly. This report has now been accepted as Irish government policy. Its underlying philosophy is that elderly people, including those with dementia, should be maintained in dignity and independence in their own homes for as long as possible if they so choose. The policy recognises the pivotal role of carers. It also recognises the stress they often suffer and the necessity to minimise this by providing a variety of services. The care service to be provided can be broadly considered under a number of headings:

(*a*) *Community support*: this means the provision and coordination of a flexible range of services to enable the sufferer to stay at home and also to support any carers involved. Such services should include general practitioners, public health nurses and home helps, while other services are meals on wheels, day care for the confused, twilight services and night sitters. Lastly, there are the community social workers and area medical officers for the elderly.

Such services will not be effective unless properly co-ordinated. Local care teams for the elderly can provide such coordination; they could also assess needs and plan for future requirements. The key figures in such teams would be area medical officers, public health nurses and community social workers.

(*b*) *Continuing care*: community care does not mean that continuing care or long-stay facilities are not required. Rather, it means that these should be provided in easily accessible, small local units in a homely atmosphere. Also, these facilities should be near relatives and friends who can continue to visit, thereby improving the quality of life of the sufferer.

This sort of care must be provided at several levels to cater for the different dependency needs of those with dementia. Firstly, there is welfare care for those requiring supervision. They may require this because they tend to wander or they need some help with washing and dressing. Then there is nursing care for those who cannot care for themselves at all or who are incontinent. Lastly, there is the more specialised care in a medical setting for those with multiple, unstable physical conditions. This sort of specialised care may also be required in a psychiatric setting for those who are grossly disturbed because of dementia.

The particular people most likely to require continuing care are those who are living alone and who are at substantial risk. The risk may exist because they constantly wander out of the house at night and get lost. Likewise, they might leave cookers on, thereby risking starting a fire. Dementia sufferers whose carers are under significant stress may also require continuing care. Again, local care teams would have a role in assessing those requiring these services and placing them in the correct environment.

(c) *Access to acute services*: it is vitally important that dementia sufferers should have easy and ready access to acute medical and psychiatric services when the need arises. Rapid treatment of medical and psychiatric problems improves the quality of life of both sufferers and carers. Five of the eight health boards, including Dublin and Cork, are fortunate in having specialist services for the elderly, termed Geriatric Medicine services. Some have developed day hospitals so that elderly people can be rapidly assessed as day patients. They can be equally rapidly treated, thereby preventing or reversing physical problems.

Specialist psychiatric services for the elderly are now being established, with the first already set up by the Eastern Health Board in North Dublin. Such services provide psychiatric assessment of dementia sufferers with associated behavioural problems in their own homes. This makes the service accessible to those who need it, mainly because if people suffer from dementia and are confused they would have great difficulty attending an outpatient clinic. In such a clinic, they would generally appear more confused than usual because they are in a strange place.

This would reduce the value of the assessment. Lastly, since the aim is to help people to stay in their homes, it is useful to see their home so its suitability can be assessed. In this way, one can obtain a better idea of how the person is managing in their home by looking around the house and asking them to carry out basic activities such as making a cup of tea.

In 1989 I set out to identify any shortcomings in the current service for elderly people, particularly those suffering from dementia. I carried out a survey of all the patients referred to my (Dublin) practice between January and June of that year. The practice is an acute psychiatric service, where about two-thirds of the patients suffer from dementia. The results are interesting.

The key findings were that public health nurses were involved with many of these patients and were assiduous in caring for them. However, the problem at times seemed to be that they were working in isolation with no clear system for dealing with problems, particularly social problems, beyond their remit. The home-help and meals-on-wheels services were widely available and much appreciated but received by relatively few. Such services also lacked flexibility since they were generally unavailable at the weekends. There was no night-time service to help with putting frail people to bed. This service could also have helped in giving medication to those with dementia who would otherwise forget to take it. There were also no sitting services to relieve carers for a few hours at night. Furthermore, day care attendance by those with dementia was extremely low, even in the areas which were well supplied with such centres. This was felt to be due to a general reluctance by some of the centres to accept people who are confused and inclined to wander. Finally, a quarter of the patients referred to this acute psychiatric service suffered only from social problems and not from behavioural or psychological problems requiring psychiatric treatment, again indicating a shortfall in community social services for those with dementia.

Clearly, there are many issues to be tackled and needs to be met for the future. Issues in the management of dementia centre around the need to obtain appropriate help for sufferers and their carers. First and foremost there is a need for people generally to be aware of dementia: who it affects, what problems it causes and how it may be dealt with. This implies a need for education which would hopefully de-stigmatise dementia and permit people to adopt a more caring, constructive attitude towards it, be they relatives, neighbours, friends or professionals.

The second issue concerns society's view of elderly people which would include those with dementia. In general terms, the elderly are not held in high esteem. Sadly, a person's value these days is measured by their job and how much they earn and own. In this context, the elderly are viewed as non-productive and 'past it' by many people. This attitude is reflected throughout society so that when it comes to planning health and social services, elderly people and particularly those with dementia are an extremely low priority group.

Thirdly, dementia sufferers are in no position to demand services for themselves. This is as a direct consequence of their disability and so others must appreciate their plight and fight for them. Their strongest advocates are the carers who look after them. There are also voluntary agencies, such as the Alzheimer's Society of Ireland and the Carers Association, who play a prominent role in educating people about dementia and in pressurising government and health boards to fund and provide services.

The next issue is the organisation of the health service itself. With its emphasis on the acute hospital services, it mitigates against the provision of decent services for the dementia sufferer. There are two aspects to this. First, it is difficult for dementia sufferers to compete for funding with glamorous acute medical services. Heart surgery seems much more important than residential care for the demented. But it is my belief that they are equally important, with both groups of patients deserving fair consideration. The fact is they both suffer if they are not managed properly.

The second aspect to our current health expenditure policy concerns what I would call 'the vicious cycle effect'. This occurs when a person with dementia runs into social difficulties at home and can no longer be supported by the available community services. In this situation, there is no proper system for dealing with the problem, the most glaring defect being the almost complete absence of community-based social workers for the elderly. The usual response is for the person to be sent to casualty by ambulance. A chest infection is the passport to admission. But when it is treated, they cannot be discharged home because they can no longer care for themselves. They then become one of the increasing band of dementia sufferers remaining in acute hospital beds because of inadequate community and residential services. The answer is obviously not to provide more acute hospital beds, but to provide proper services in the community.

Another problem that frequently concerns carers is handling the assets of their dementing relative. In Ireland there are two ways in which people can take charge of the assets of a relative: power of attorney and ward of court. Power of attorney involves someone with the help of his solicitor giving power to a relative to manage his money and property. To give power of attorney, a person must be mentally capable and it is only valid if the person remains mentally capable. Obviously, this cannot be used as a mechanism to handle the affairs of a dementing relative. The only option is to make a person a ward of court.

The ward of court procedure is a lengthy one, involving the President of the High Court. Two medical opinions must be obtained to say that the person is mentally incapable of managing his own affairs. If the person is taken into wardship, a committee is then appointed which may include a relative to manage the person's affairs. My description alone will, I think, give you a flavour of the complexity of the whole procedure. A far more satisfactory solution would be to have an enduring power of attorney as in the UK. This allows a person to give power of attorney to a relative while they are still mentally capable, and they are likely to be mentally capable in the early stages of dementia. The power of attorney would continue to operate when the person was no longer mentally capable. In this way, the need for ward of court proceedings would be circumvented.

There are two more issues I would like to address before ending this paper. Firstly, the recent announcement by the government of a carer's allowance is a major landmark, in my opinion. This is so because it formally acknowledges the responsibility that health and welfare services have to the chronically disabled. This is a welcome shift from the emphasis on acute hospital services. I hope that the carer's allowance will not be so stringently means-tested that it excludes that group of women, namely, housewives, who play such an important part in supporting their dementing relatives at home.

The second issue concerns the abuse of people suffering from dementia by their carers. Abuse of the elderly — like child abuse ten to fifteen years ago — is increasingly being recognised as a problem. The elderly demented have been identified as one of the groups most likely to be abused. The abuse can be either physical or mental, or can involve withholding necessary medication or abusing the person's finances. In most cases, the abuse occurs as a consequence of enormous stress in the carer and obviously should be tackled by reducing the stress. In a few cases, the abuse is carried out by what is termed a pathological carer: that is, some-thing in the carer's make-up causes him to act in this way.

The usual causes of pathological abuse is that the carer abuses alcohol, suffers from a mental disorder or comes from the sort of family in which violence is a common occurrence. In these cases, there is no mechanism for protecting the dementia sufferer, and this is quite unlike the situation that arises when a child is the victim. I mention this issue to bring it to wider attention and to suggest that there is a need for a statutory mechanism to manage this problem. It is necessary because, like children, dementia sufferers cannot protect themselves from such abuse.

In conclusion, a few points should be emphasised. It must be recognised that dementia is a common problem among elderly people in Ireland and will become increasingly more common because of the trend for people to live longer. Tragically, young people will continue to be affected in the years to come. However, it is vital to stress that dementia is nothing to be ashamed of. It is a condition with a physical cause and it is not contagious. If you suspect that a relative has it, then early medical help and a positive diagnosis can contribute significantly towards planning for the sufferer's future.

It is important for those not directly involved to be aware of dementia too. This terrible condition is not helped by people being so frightened by it that they try to ignore it or lock the afflicted away. Dementia sufferers are vulnerable and their carers are under enormous stress. Their suffering can be reduced if they are cared for in a way that will maintain their dignity despite the loss of dignity that results from a condition like dementia. Providing adequate services is an integral part of treating people with respect. For the future, I would hope to see such services developing hand in hand with an increasing awareness in Ireland of dementia and the problems it brings for both sufferers and their carers.

SEVEN

Crime and Mental Disorder

Art O'Connor

Several years ago a man in his late twenties was released from an Irish prison having served most of a ten-year sentence for rape. The rape was a particularly savage one and the rapist was noted to be a very violent and aggressive young man. Shortly after his release he moved to the UK, where he struck again. This time he attacked and killed his victim. He was eventually convicted of murder and is now serving a sentence of life imprisonment in England.

This is just one example of the real-life crime dramas that have appeared in Irish headlines in recent decades. Brutal crimes against women and especially sex offences against children commonly hit the news. We have also seen frequent accounts of murder trials where men have killed their wives, girlfriends or acquaintances. Given the nature of the acts involved, it is understandable if we sometimes ask whether the perpetrators of these crimes are mad or mentally ill in some way. It is this association between mental illness and crime that is the subject of this paper.

I will begin be examining the kinds of criminal activity that are associated with some of the major forms of mental disorder. Many different types of mental illness and mental disorder arise in my day-to-day clinical experience. The first is *manic-depressive psychosis*. The commonest form of this disorder is an episode or a series of episodes of serious depression. This is where the person's mood is very depressed and he or she can lose all interest in life. The sufferer may stop eating and lose considerable amounts of weight. Serious sleeping problems and feelings of worth-lessness and guilt can be features as well. Depression is considered by many specialists to be the commonest associated psychiatric disorder in homicide cases. Occasionally in Ireland we see cases where a person decides to kill his or her family and then commit suicide. In one such case, a man believed that he and his family were going to suffer great shame and misery because of financial loss and poverty. This belief was a delusion and was based on his serious mental depression. His plan was to kill his children, then his wife and, finally, himself. However, he succeeded only in killing one of the children and was subsequently charged with murder. He was found guilty but insane because he was judged to be not responsible for his actions at the time of the killing.

The other form of manic-depressive psychosis is where the person's mood is raised and he is elated. Here, the person is full of energy, needs to keep moving, ideas flood into his mind and he must keep talking non-stop. During this disturbance, a man's sex drive can be increased and occasionally we come across sex offences committed by the manic man. One particular case we came across was of a young man who was being treated in a hospital for his mania and had an argument with another patient. The other patient died following a blow from the manic patient. He was also found guilty but insane because it was viewed by the court that he was not responsible for his actions. Overall, manic-depressive psychosis is only occasionally seen in association with crime, but it is a real association, nevertheless.

The second mental illness I will examine is *schizophrenia*. This is probably the most serious psychiatric illness and it accounts for most of the psychiatric bed occupancy throughout the country. There are various forms of it. Some have an acute course; others have a relapsing course; and some more have a chronic effect on the sufferer. The person frequently becomes withdrawn from the world and can lose contact with his or her surroundings and with reality. Auditory hallucinations — which are often persecutory — are a frequent feature. So are delusions. These delusions are false, fixed beliefs that often take the form of persecutory ideas involving people who conspire against the person or try to harm him in some way.

The typical crime committed by the schizophrenic involves stealing food from a supermarket because he cannot look after himself. From time to time we come across a case where a person with schizophrenia goes into a restaurant and has a meal, but is unable to pay. This can happen repeatedly and the courts sometimes feel they have no option but to incarcerate the person for a period of time. Again, sex offences are occasionally seen in association with schizophrenia and sometimes the victim can be elderly.

Overall, serious crime is generally rare among schizophrenics, but sometimes arson and homicide can be seen. Such offences may be related to the auditory hallucinations which order the person to commit the offence. They may also be related to delusions that someone is persecuting him and he feels that he must strike out to protect himself.

Sometimes a man has a delusion that his wife is having an affair. He may then try to kill the supposed lover because of this delusion, and the target or victim may be completely unaware of the mentally ill person's beliefs. Alternatively, the schizophrenic man with delusions of infidelity may kill his wife instead.

Female patients also present with schizophrenic delusions. I once treated a woman in her sixties who believed that a spaceship was orbiting the earth and was about to take her up to heaven. She wanted her grand-children to go with her, but she believed that she had to kill them to achieve this. The tragic outcome was that she killed her three grand-children with a knife one evening while she was babysitting. Such cases may be rare, but they occasionally come to our attention.

Personality disorder is my third example of mental illness. Strictly speaking, this is not a mental illness at all, but is an abnormality that can cause the person to come into contact with the psychiatric services. The person may have difficulty coping with life and have serious problems with relationships. They may be involved in law-breaking and this can sometimes be seen from the early teens. Alcohol and drug abuse may also be a feature in cases of personality disorder; so also are suicide attempts. Overall, poor family backgrounds are a frequent feature, as is deprivation of various kinds.

It is my experience that virtually all types of offences can arise in association with the seriously disordered personality. However, personality disorders are especially linked to crimes of violence. Sometimes, morbid jealousy can be identified and patients can be seriously violent to their wives or to others whom they believe to be their wives' lovers. Other forms of serious violence can be committed by those with personality disorders, especially sex offences.

In the 1960s the psychiatric world was very optimistic about the treatment of people with disordered personalities. Treatments such as those in the Henderson Hospital in London and Grendon Prison in Southern England grew as a result. However, the enthusiasm that started these units has waned over the years and most psychiatrists no longer treat personality disorders *per se*. Instead, they try to help these people with their alcohol abuse, their drug abuse, symptoms of depression or other disorders.

The association between schizophrenia, manic-depressive psychosis, personality disorders and criminal activity is certainly real, although not always common. I will next examine the association between crime and mental disorder by looking at the various types of offences involved. Because it seems most likely that mental disorder is more frequently associated with serious crime, I think we should look at two main categories of this type of crime: namely, homicide and sex offences.

It is estimated that about 30 per cent of perpetrators of homicide have a serious psychiatric problem. Schizophrenia is seen in some of these. We can also find depressions and other disorders including alcoholism. Where schizophrenia is involved, the person may be acting in response to persecutory delusions or auditory hallucinations. He or she may believe that their partner is trying to administer poison or is trying to beam some ray that is going to kill. The mentally ill person may feel so frightened and under threat that they see no alternative but to kill the other person in self-defence. The unfortunate victim may not realise that any of this turmoil is going on in the other person's mind.

Interestingly, if the victim of the homicide is a parent, then it is very likely that the perpetrator suffers from schizophrenia. This is confirmed in various research projects in the UK and the US which examined male subjects who kill a parent. It is confirmed in female subjects who kill a parent in a UK study that Paul d'Orban and myself completed last year.

The common situation is that the mentally ill and deluded patient lives alone with the elderly parent. The ill person can be under stress for a long time, with the result that he or she is barely able to cope. The parent can be perceived as nagging and constantly making little of the patient. In a final burst of anger related to frustration the patient kills the parent.

The same scenario can occur if the patient suffers from a depressive disorder, although it is highly uncommon. One eighteen-year-old woman I encountered several years ago suffered from post-natal depression. Her father was dead. But her mother, who was elderly, frequently berated and criticised her. This resulted in the daughter experiencing a fit of utter frustration related to her depressive disorder and the stress of the recent childbirth. She killed her mother while she slept, using a hammer. Her case is one of the rare examples where the perpetrator of the parent's homicide is not schizophrenic. She made a good recovery from her depression.

Alcohol is a further issue which we must consider when examining the phenomenon of homicide. In homicide cases it seems that about 60 per cent of the perpetrators are intoxicated at the time of the murder. Interestingly, approximately 30 per cent of the victims are also intoxicated. To take an example, one very dependent man in his late twenties became very unhappy and distressed throughout the six months that his marriage was breaking up. He and his partner had a young baby, but he strongly believed that his partner was being influenced by friends in their neighbourhood. He drank heavily for several months and then, in a fit of despair, drank constantly for several hours. Finally, he downed a full bottle of whiskey. In this very intoxicated state he went to the house where his wife had started to live with her friends. He pleaded with her to come home. When she refused he lunged at her with a knife. He was totally open about his offence and has repeated ever since that 'I have killed the only person I have ever loved.'

As mentioned earlier, morbid jealousy is sometimes seen in association with homicide. In particular, this type of very unreasonable and possessive jealousy can be seen in association with alcoholism. The person may believe that his wife is having an affair with another man. He disregards all evidence to the contrary. He may come home at night, intoxicated, and find that he is unable to get an erection. This he believes is further evidence of his wife's infidelity. His wife may refuse to go to bed with him and have sex because of his drunken state. Again, he explains this on the basis that she is involved with a lover. The jealousy syndrome can be related to mental illness or personality disorder. It is sometimes known as the Othello syndrome, a reference to Shakespeare's Othello who becomes morbidly jealous of his wife in response to Iago's trickery.

The question of the insanity defence to murder has been highlighted by the media following the prosecution of a number of well-known cases by the courts. In Ireland the insanity defence is concerned with what are called 'The McNaughton Rules', named after Daniel McNaughton, who in 1843 tried to kill the leader of the Tory Party, Sir Robert Peel, because he believed he was being persecuted by him. He failed to kill Sir Robert, but killed his secretary by mistake. He was found not guilty by reason of insanity. There was a public outcry at the time, with the result that the House of Lords set several questions for judges in an attempt to clarify the position concerning insanity. The result has been known as the McNaughton Rules and they form the basis of the insanity defence in the UK, Ireland and the US.

The McNaughton Rules firstly presume that the defendants are sane until proven otherwise. For the defence to be successful they stipulate that the person must have suffered from a 'disease of the mind'. Furthermore, the person must not have known the 'nature and quality of his act' or, if he did know this, he did not know that it was wrong. Essentially, by 'disease of the mind' is meant the psychiatric illnesses such as schizophrenia or depression, but it can also mean mental handicap, dementia and epilepsy.

These rules are very restrictive and, ironically, even Daniel McNaughton would not have qualified under them. Therefore, a third limb was added following the Hayes case in the 1960s and the Dorricott case in 1983. In effect, it allows for the position where a person who is suffering from a disease of the mind could not exercise 'free will' over his actions at the time of the offence. This, in other words, is similar to the concept of 'irresistible impulse', which can therefore be used as a defence. This has widened the scope of the rules.

Unlike in Ireland, the defence of 'diminished responsibility' has been used in the United Kingdom since the

Homicide Act of 1957. This defence allows for the concept of admitting some — but not all — mental responsibility in murder charges. It must be shown that the person's responsibility was 'substantially reduced' because of an abnormality of mind. If this is successful the charge is reduced to manslaughter and the judge can deal with the case as he sees fit. This can mean prison, a hospital order or even probation.

By comparison, if insanity is found in Ireland the judge has no discretion. He must commit the person to the Central Mental Hospital at the pleasure of the court. This can mean for a long time. The fact that the system is so restrictive and hidebound can create many anomalies. It is my opinion that we could well learn from the UK and introduce a less restrictive form of insanity defence, similar to diminished responsibility, in this country.

The second major category of serious offences concerns those of a sexual nature. Here, the associations between crime and mental illness are not so clear. In rape, for instance, there is a very low incidence of mental illness among the perpetrators. But in a proportion of cases the rapist is a person with a seriously anti-social personality disorder and a history of violence and previous offending.

There are many facts that we do know about rape as a crime. For example, the victims and assailants know each other in about 30 per cent of cases. Also, alcohol is often involved and a proportion of victims are also intoxicated at the time of the offence. Lastly, it is estimated that about 20 per cent of rape cases involve more than one assailant.

In a proportion of rape cases we encounter men who have a deep-seated hatred of women and sometimes even a fear of them. Obviously their crime is a sexual one, but it is more than that. Sexual fantasy and lust are often precursors to a serious sex offence. So also is the urge to be violent and to dominate another human being. From time to time we find mental illness associated with rape. One example is the case of a schizophrenic who rapes an elderly woman, or the manic patient who indecently assaults a person in his state of extreme arousal. Overall, however, the links between rape and mental illness are hard to establish.

Indecent exposure is probably the commonest sex offence. But again, mental illness is rarely the cause. The indecent exposer is often a person who is afraid of women and who has difficulties in social settings with female company. It has been postulated that the exhibitionist has deep-seated sexual insecurities and fears for his own masculinity. He exposes his penis to a woman in order that she be frightened by it. This seems to make him feel that he really is a man and brings reassurance for a period of time. There is a strong compulsive element to this type of offending and soon after exposing himself to a victim he wants to repeat the performance. Some describe mounting stress and tension that is only relieved by the very act of indecently exposing the penis.

As in the case of indecent exposure, mental illness is also rare among the incest offender and the paedophile. Some sexual assaults by fathers can involve very minor sexual activity such as touching, but can progress to very serious sexual assault such as rape. It is difficult to know what is in the incestuous father's mind. Some would claim they are in fact loving their child. Of course, this claim would be rejected by the normal person who would see it as a gross distortion of the reality of sexual abuse and breach of trust. Secondly, alcohol problems are frequently seen among incestuous fathers. Lastly, sexual motivation and the motivation of dominating another human being are probably the real motivating factors behind a father's sexual assaults.

So far, I have concentrated on male sex offenders. And although we seldom hear about sex offences committed by women, they certainly do occur. There have been no major studies undertaken in Ireland. However, in 1987 I completed a research project on this very issue in London's Holloway Prison. I concluded that the majority of women involved in sex offences were not mentally ill and were usually convicted of aiding and abetting a sexual offence. Only a small number were diagnosed as schizophrenic or suffering from manic-depressive psychosis. The results would be highly applicable to this country.

In one case, a fifty-year-old woman who had a serious alcohol problem and was separated, allowed her twelve-year-old daughter to have sex with an older male friend of hers. She permitted this in return for money for a holiday. This happened on several occasions. She was sentenced to one year's imprisonment and her male friend was given a suspended sentence because of ill-health. In another case, a woman allowed her twelve-year-old daughter to be raped by the stepfather. She participated in this assault and said it was to punish the girl for bad behaviour. This explanation seemed bizarre and inhuman. She was given a two-year prison sentence and the man a longer term.

There are no comparable studies for this country. But in my clinical experience it is clear that female sex offences are very rare indeed. There certainly have been a few cases in Ireland in recent years where females were suspected of committing such offences, but no charges were ever brought against these people, as far as I am aware.

To conclude, I want to concentrate a little on prevention, especially prevention of serious crime. It is the role of psychiatrists to try to identify mentally ill patients who are a danger to themselves or to others. In this way, we hope that the early detection of mental illness, such as schizophrenia and serious depression, can prevent serious violent crimes such as homicide. Prompt action is sometimes required in terms of treatment or admission to hospital if we feel such people's symptoms are deteriorating. Close follow-up is also required where there is a history of serious violence or where jealousy is a major part of the mental illness process.

Unfortunately, there are reasons why these goals cannot always be achieved. Some killings that are perpetrated by mentally ill people are not predictable, so there is little the psychiatrist can do. Secondly, most murderers are not mentally ill and so the prevention of such killings is more a sociological or criminological dilemma than a psychiatric one. Lastly, with sex offences there is a much looser association between the offences and mental illness. This means that symptoms of mental illness alone cannot help us in prediction or prevention.

There are, however, some measures we can take to prevent re-offending. For a start, some groups of sex offenders might benefit from group therapy, at least in the longer term. We have started such a programme for incest offenders in the National Forensic Psychiatric Service in Ireland and it has been running for over a year now. We can also help the offender who is a paedophile and offending against children outside the home. In this case, drugs which temporarily reduce or wipe out his sex drive are the only sure way of preventing re-offending.

A third and final area where re-offending may be prevented concerns young offenders in their teens, who have emotional problems. We come across many of these young men who have interpersonal problems, family difficulties, educational and other deprivations and little social support. They can start off with minor offending and some go on to more serious and violent crime.

We run a programme on an outpatient basis for a limited number of young offenders, and research on this programme shows that re-offending is reduced in this group, at least while they are attending the programme. This may be one area where more developments nationally would show benefits, both for society and for potential offenders. By helping this vulnerable group we can break the link between mental disorder and criminal behaviour in at least proportion of offenders in this country. It is a small but effective step in the right direction.

EIGHT

Depression in Ireland

Patrick McKeon

The grieving father's lament for his favourite son is a story heard all too often in the Ireland of today. It is the story of a father asking why his son had to kill himself. 'Why did he die at a time when everything he had worked so hard for in life had come his way: a college degree, a prestigious job, the future ahead looking bright and a family and friends so close and so caring?' As his father so plaintively asks, 'Why didn't he tell somebody? Why didn't he talk to me? It was depression — if only I had known.' Each year this tragic story is all too frequently repeated in towns and cities throughout Ireland. This story is the ultimate tragic consequence of a condition called 'depression'.

It may be shocking to hear that over 10,000 admissions to psychiatric hospital each year are diagnosed as having a depressive illness. Overall, some 200,000 Irish people suffer from depression right now, and that estimate is based on community figures in other countries which we have no reason to believe would be different in Ireland. To take another statistic: one in three Irish people had either suffered from depression or had a family member or close friend treated for depression, according to a recent national survey conducted by AWARE, the depression support group. Lastly, only one in ten of all those who suffer from depression receive treatment; so while it is a hidden condition it is not totally so, at least for the 10 per cent who seek help.

Depression is a normal experience; it is in a sense the mind's equivalent of what the body calls pain or hurt. Just as we have a normal body temperature or heart rate, so too we have a normal range of mood swings within which we can experience the everyday ups and downs. We regard this as a normal range, in that everybody experiences it and we can cope with these highs and lows of everyday living. However, when the mood changes are more than the person can cope with, then the depression is considered to have moved into the realms of an abnormal or clinical mood disturbance. But as doctors do not have the equivalent of a thermometer to detect an abnormal depression, they have to rely on the individual's ability to recognise the shift from normality.

As might be expected, most do recognise this shift in mood from what was their previous norm. This recognition is prompted by the increasing difficulties they have in coping with their everyday lives. However, they frequently will not see the shift with the same glaring clarity as they would see the mercury rise in a thermometer when they have a fever. Furthermore, the shift from normal mood change to clinical depression is often not recognised as such, but is seen as an extreme fatigue, insomnia, poor concentration or bodily complaints. It is left to the family or the general practitioner to diagnose these changes as depression.

It is worth asking, however, if you can easily tell if somebody suffers from depression. This precise question was indeed asked in the AWARE national survey referred to earlier, and about half of those interviewed disagreed while the remainder believed that, yes, you could easily recognise depression in others. In reality, however, being able to identify it will depend on how well you know the person and the severity of the condition. The fact is that depression, except in its more severe form, can be hidden from all except those with whom the person lives and even then it can be disguised for a time. So when we cannot see depression, it is not simply as William Osler said that 'half of us are blind, few of us feel and we are all deaf', but that the sufferer chooses to conceal his or her plight.

And hide it they certainly do. Parents, close relatives, friends, employers and work colleagues can be fooled by the cheerful façade. For example, a study of what employees tell their boss about depression was conducted by the Depression Research Unit at St Patrick's Hospital, Dublin. This study found that whether the person had received treatment in a psychiatric hospital, at an outpatients' clinic, or from their general practitioner, the majority have concealed, would conceal and would advise others to conceal their depression. Even those whose employers know of their depression will continue to request their doctors to enter a diagnosis other than a psychiatric one on their medical certificates.

According to surveys of public attitudes to mental illness, society is more tolerant of aberrant behaviour when it is not described as a form of, or attributable to, mental disorder. For example, AWARE's study of Irish public attitudes revealed that 60 per cent of people do not consider depression to be a form of mental illness, while a much lower figure of 20 per cent considered it to be so. A further indication of increasing public acceptance of depressive illness is that the depressed, in this study, were neither viewed as being of weak character, nor as feeling sorry for themselves, by two-thirds of those interviewed.

Even when it came to the possibility of direct and even intimate contact with people who have depression, the majority of the Irish public expressed a willingness to have such contact. This extended to relationships with employees, child minders or even marriage partners. Comparing the AWARE survey with that of the Mental Health Association of Ireland conducted in 1973, it appears that the general public of 1990 is much more likely to employ or marry someone who has suffered from depression or manic-depression than it was in 1973.

These encouraging changes in public perception probably mean little to the depressed, particularly when low. And the notion of exposing themselves as being weak or inadequate, or the prospect of being told to 'snap out of it', can be daunting. In practice, most depressives, even when they have recovered, are loath to divulge their secret. Only when they can no longer hide their suffering because they have been hospitalised, or have had lengthy periods of sick leave from work, will their secret surface.

The silent majority, largely composed of the nine out of ten who do not have treatment, carry their burden in private, and as such their experience never becomes incorporated into the public's perception of what depression is. As a result, the dividing line between having and not having a depressive illness is going to be perceived by the public as a very stark one, being, as they are, unaware of the different gradations of depression.

In this century personal revelations of depression have come from the pens of writers, novelists, playwrights and biographers, all of whom have given graphic accounts of their depressions. Sylvia Plath, Virginia Woolf, Ernest Hemingway, Eugene O'Neill, Brendan Behan and Robert Lowell could not have explored the universe of their minds without having some of their personal sufferings come into public view. Politicians, too, have helped, at least those who could afford it, to dent the image of the depressive as a weak-natured, pitiful being, by laying open their emotional life to biographers and historians. Winston Churchill in later life spoke of his depression thus: 'When I was young, for two or three years the light faded out of the picture. I did my work. I sat in the House of Commons, but black depression settled on me. Even now, I don't like standing near the edge of a platform when an express train is passing through — a second's action would end everything.' Churchill, the personification of valour for people all over the world, was also a human being, and his bouts of depression had not diminished his greatness but added to his humanity. Leaders of stature who have faced the enemy of depression within, people such as Franklin Delano Roosevelt, Mao Tse-tung and

Harold Macmillan, seem to have fared best against the enemy without.

In more recent times in Ireland Johnny McEvoy, Eoghan Harris and Brenda Fricker have given the lead to countless others. But these enlightened few who could either choose to wear their depression in public or who, because it was so obvious, could not conceal it, are a tiny minority. It is the silent majority — the employed and unemployed, the bosses and the workers, the teachers and the nurses, the mechanics and the designers, the young and the elderly — who hold the missing pieces of the jigsaw to complete the picture of what depression truly is.

There are many misconceptions about depression, including some amazing views about what causes these mood disturbances. For example, the much talked about association between unemployment and depression — for which there is rather flimsy research evidence — was only mentioned by 5 per cent of people in AWARE's national survey. Top ranking as a cause was given by the public to stress in interpersonal relationships and pressure at work. Bereavement was the next most frequently mentioned as a cause. Genetic factors were ranked third and, interestingly, more particularly so by farmers, rural dwellers and the elderly. This may reflect the fact that they live in a more stable environment with few, if any, changes of family residence for decades or even centuries. As a result, they have a unique chance to observe inherited genetic characteristics through the generations. These observations, coupled with a farmer's first-hand experience of the effect of breeding on the temperament of animals, may account for their views. Difficult childhood experiences were the fourth most frequently mentioned cause in the survey. Finally, 1 per cent cited either loneliness, bad health, post-natal depression or drink problems as relevant causes.

The public's perceptions of the different causes of clinical depression are surprisingly accurate. Depression seen by the general practitioner is more likely to result from distressing life events, be they bereavement, relationship problems or career disappointments. Such reactive depressions are understandable, in that we could all imagine ourselves being equally depressed if we should experience similar losses. Personality factors are also of relevance here, in that some less robust individuals will be less able to tolerate loss and distress in life than others.

However there is a second grouping of depressions, namely the endogenous or internal depressions and manic-depressions, and these are loosely referred to as biological depressions. These can come totally out of the blue or are precipitated by relatively minor mishaps. They are frequently found to run in families, to be more severe than the reactive forms and by their very nature to tend to recur, often on a seasonal basis. Psychiatrists either at outpatients' clinics or in a hospital setting are more likely to be dealing with these severe biological depressions.

Studies indicate that over 40 per cent of people hospitalised with depression cannot identify any distressing life event that might account for their mood disturbance. A substantial body of research indicates that these biological disorders, in particular manic-depression, have strong genetic aspects: for example, the immediate relatives of people with manic-depression have a fifteen times greater chance than average of being treated for a similar mood disorder, while an identical twin of an individual with manic-depression has a 70 per cent chance of having a similar disorder.

So far this paper has examined the causes and the different forms of depression, together with the public perceptions of the condition. Now to the treatment of depression, firstly to some of the findings from the AWARE public survey referred to earlier. For a start, the AWARE survey found that, when asked if depression could be successfully treated, three out of four people believed it could. Significantly, more people in the higher socio-economic groups and those living in Dublin considered depression to be treatable than did unskilled workers and rural dwellers. But a particularly worrying finding was that people aged over sixty-five tended to believe that depression simply had to be lived with and that there was no worthwhile treatment.

When those who considered depression to be treatable were asked how depression should be treated, one-third recommended counselling, one in four recommended antidepressant medication and one in five considered talking to a family member or close friend. Again, we see a remarkable degree of concurrence with present-day research evidence. For example, recent studies emphasised the value of combining counselling with antidepressant medication. Again, sociologist George Brown and his colleagues in their London study in the late 1970s clearly demonstrated that women who did not have somebody close to confide in were significantly more vulnerable to depression.

Other interesting findings to emerge from the AWARE survey were that single women in particular mentioned counselling as their preferred choice, as did those in the upper socio-economic groups, while tablets were ranked highest as a worthwhile treatment by farmers and rural dwellers. Again, the elderly considered admission to a psychiatric hospital as the preferred treatment for depression.

Of two worrying findings from this study, one was particularly alarming in that only one in every six people mentioned their general practitioner as a means of getting help for depression, in a country where most first-line psychiatric care is given by general practitioners. By way of contrast, 41 per cent of those surveyed in 1973 nominated their GP as the appropriate person to contact for mental health purposes. It is unclear whether this public perception is a reflection of the problems that GPs have in recognising depression, in the time constraints that are the cross of the busy GP, or perhaps it is indicative of the changing nature of the doctor/patient relationship in present-day Irish society. The other cause for concern is that 7 per cent of the population still reckon that people with depression should simply 'cop on'.

Before leaving this survey, I would like to point out one problem that the survey could not address, and that is, how the different forms of depression, with their different causes, required different treatments. A bout of depression which is solely determined by a major loss is best treated with counselling, whereas a recurring endogenous or manic-depressive illness is highly unlikely to benefit from any treatment other than antidepressant medication, or mood stabilising drugs. This critical difference is not sufficiently understood by the public.

Before concluding, it is essential to turn to the most serious consequence of depression, namely, suicide. The suicide rate, often thought to be particularly low in Ireland, has increased in the past five years. The Central Statistics Office figures show that there are over 200 suicides in Ireland annually. However, Dr Clarke-Finegan and Professor Tom Fahy's study in Galway clearly demonstrated that the actual suicide rate is three to four times higher than the official figure indicates. Psychiatrists around the country echo one another's concern about the increasing number of suicides amongst their patients. Dr Michael Kelleher and his colleagues in Cork, as a result of their surveys, have tended to incriminate the increasing pressures of modern living, especially amongst teenagers and young adults. They have also pointed to the disintegration of the extended family network and the diminishing influence of religion as a stabilising and cohesive influence in society as contributing factors.

Another aspect, yet to be addressed in Ireland, is the influence of newspaper and other media reports of suicide deaths. The American sociologist, D.P. Phillips, found that in the period immediately following suicide publicity, the number of suicide deaths increased for a short period following the publicity. The highest rates were in the geographical areas nearest to the incident and in the regions most exposed to the newspaper publicity. Other research indicates that knowing how a person, particularly a family member, committed suicide substantially increases the risk of a suicide in somebody with severe depression.

So, with an increasing liberalisation of attitudes to suicide, is there a corresponding increase in the suicide rate? The Phillips studies and those of Dr Kelleher and his colleagues in Cork have highlighted the phenomenon of copycat suicides. But these studies need to be extended to see if media coverage of suicide events can be used to the opposite effect, thereby reducing the incidence of fatal outcomes. To date, most suicide publicity has focussed on the details of the method used by the victim, while the pain and anguish of the bereaved family is hidden from public view. Could it be that emphasising the distress of their grief would redress any imbalance that might exist in current reporting practices and so provide some antidote to the contagion of suicidal behaviour?

I began this paper with the story of a father now coping with his son's tragic death by suicide. It is the story of a son who knew he was seriously depressed, had attended a psychiatrist and was having treatment for two weeks prior to his death. What we also know is that his father's mother had manic-depression and that he had had a row with his girlfriend, leading to a temporary separation some months prior to the onset of his depression. His father pondered this information as he sat in the room where his son spent his final hours. As his father looked out at the recently repaired window, images of how his son must have felt in his last moments went tumbling through his mind. Did he not think of those he left behind, his father, his mother, his sisters, his girlfriend, his many friends? He loved life so much, did it not beckon him back from the window's edge? Why did he not tell us that he was depressed? Even his doctor's advice went unheeded. We would have understood, we could have saved him.

The grieving father's reverberating questions grind to a halt as he realises the very reasons his son could not talk about his depression. For he, too, would have seen depression as a condition of the weak-willed and of those who lack determination and moral fibre. No, he would not have told his family, friends or employers about his depression. What his son never knew, nor his wife or children, was that he, too, had suffered from a bout of depression in his late twenties when working in England. He, too, had looked into the abyss of death and only a spell in hospital saved him from a fate similar to that of his son. He can recall the sense of shame and humiliation, the fear of being thought of as a lesser man and how he went to extreme lengths to hide his problem from his parents. In the agonising tyranny of depression the wonder is not that so many people kill themselves, but that so few do. Those who come through unscathed would say that having somebody there who cares, somebody whom they can confide in, somebody whom they could not bear to hurt by a suicidal act, is the thing that keeps them alive.

We live in changing times. Recently we saw the crumbling of the Berlin Wall, the dismantling of the Iron Curtain and the quiet revolution in Eastern Europe. There is an air of freedom about, blowing from the East and from Africa. We witness a unity of purpose, a sense of global concern for our planet and those who inhabit it. At home, too, there is an increasing awareness of some of the marginalised groups in our society: the travellers, homo-sexuals, incest victims and the handicapped. This new tolerance is mirrored in the caring and compassionate and well-informed attitudes expressed by Irish people today for those with depression.

So we could ask if Irish society has at long last reached maturity? It certainly seems well disposed to those who suffer from depression and seems ready to welcome them out of the closet of secrecy. To date, we have had the Johnny McEvoys, the Eoghan Harrises and the Brenda

Frickers of this world. What we now need are the silent majority, the foot-soldiers of life. It will be the O'Sullivans, the Murphys, the O'Connors of this country — the nameless ones — who will rid their fellow sufferers of the stigma of depression and, as Abraham Lincoln put it, 'Give freedom to the slaves and assure freedom to the free.'

NINE

Alcohol Excess — the curse of the drinking classes

Marcus Webb

Alcohol and all of life that surrounds it provide a topic which touches every person in Ireland. Experts abound, from the brewer and the publican to the total abstainer and the twopence-ha'penny politician on the bar stool. Alcohol percolates through our social structures and influences family relationships, recreation, cultural life, working efficiency and hospital and prison statistics. We use alcohol for celebration and for softening sorrows, for relaxation and to give courage, for cementing commercial agreements and for loosening artistic expression. We often rejoice with alcohol at the start of a new life, but drinking contributes to too many deaths. It is used to highlight family reunions, including marriages, but causes other families to disintegrate. Alcohol plays its part in religious ritual, but also in loutish and brutal profanities.

My own perspective is as a psychiatrist and inevitably I see the darker side of alcohol in Irish life. But as an individual I can enjoy a social drink with family and friends and experience its pleasurable tranquillising effects on the brain. For alcohol is a drug; make no mistake about it. It is a drug with widespread effects on the brain and, indeed, on other organs of the body. It is a depressant drug, not a stimulant, but its depressing effects on higher brain function can go beyond reducing social unease to release more basic and less acceptable behaviour.

So, to refer to the title of my talk: with due acknowledgment to Oscar Wilde, the curse of the drinking classes
is not work, in this context, but is the ease with which
drinking can become excessive. Human social life can be
said to involve choices and balance of tension between
moderation and excess, although some people have fewer
options and less control over their lives than others. Little
boys are expected to learn to be manly but not aggressive,
little girls to be feminine but not submissive. Young
employees may be ambitious but not pushy; even the
clergy may quite reasonably be holy, but are not listened
to if they are sanctimonious.

So it is with our society's handling of alcohol. If we
wish to use a psychoactive drug so widely we must learn
to use it moderately, and to limit its damaging effects.
Alcohol has probably been the most widely used recreational drug throughout the world since the Stone Age,
although many other substances such as opium, mescaline,
cocaine, caffeine, nicotine and cannabis have been and still
are used for similar purposes. Like alcohol in the West,
such drugs have often achieved prominence in religious
rituals, but have also developed everyday meaning in
medical, commercial, festive and recreational contexts. If
our National Drugs Advisory Board were to consider a
new application from a pharmaceutical firm to market
alcohol as, say, a minor tranquilliser it would without any
hesitation turn it down. For alcohol has far too many
adverse effects, and the margin between its desired and its
unwanted effects is much too narrow. In particular, it
readily produces addiction in those who use it excessively.
Yet alcohol is available, at a modest price compared to many
drugs, over the counter of thousands of retail premises
throughout the country.

The earliest evidence relating to alcohol in Ireland is
archaeological, coming from the discovery of funerary
vessels dated to the early Bronze Age, between 1800 and
2000 BC, wherein traces of a type of beer were found. The

beverage was strongly flavoured by myrtle berries, perhaps to conceal its crude and unpleasant taste. The Celts almost certainly brought wine from Southern Continental Europe. They have been described from earliest Greek writings as a people who were given to enjoying themselves: passionate, warm and imaginative, impressionable and superstitious. Plato noted that the Celts were drunken and combative. How many of these attributes the more recent Irish have inherited or held on to from particular Celtic forebears, and to what extent these matters are related to modern Irish drinking patterns, must be open to question. However, there did develop, probably as early as the fifteenth century in Ireland, what might be called a strong weakness for distilled spirits, whiskey in particular, at a time when the English were more attracted to wines, ales, mead and cider. Travellers told of the widespread role that drinking played in the lives of Irish people; drunkenness was common and there appeared to be few strictures on its use. Porter and also the illicit *poitin* began to become popular in the eighteenth and nineteenth centuries. Over 16,000 *poitin* stills, for example, were discovered and confiscated in 1833–4.

In England, Scotland and Wales heavy drinking and drunkenness were also common, the more so after the Puritans lost power with the Restoration of Charles II in 1660. During the eighteenth and nineteenth centuries in Ireland, as well as in industrial England, effective membership of the various occupational groups required heavy drinking. Men were hired and wages were commonly paid in public houses, and both workingmen's political groups and local entertainments were to be found only in the drinking houses. Fair days were and still are marked in Ireland by extensive drinking as bargains are discussed, pursued, sealed or regretted.

Sociologists have pointed to the importance of the attitudes taken up by the prevailing religion, and it has been observed that the stricter Protestant, Nonconformist

Churches tended to see great evil in drink, while the Catholic Church has usually taken a more charitable view of drunkenness than of other human frailties.

However, modern Ireland has been described as having an ambivalent cultural attitude to drinking, rather than a permissive one. This is because of the remarkable number of total abstainers co-existing in the country alongside the 75 per cent of the adult population who drink. Seventeen per cent are said to be lifetime abstainers, and 7 per cent abstainers who formerly drank. By comparison, England and Wales have only 8.5 per cent abstainers. The Temperance Movement began in the early nineteenth century in Skibbereen and then in New Ross, mainly at the instigation of the Quakers. They campaigned for moderation in drinking rather than total abstinence and paved the way for the much more successful campaigns centred on Father Mathew and later on Father Cullen.

Mathew was a charismatic figure who appealed to the ordinary people, aiming to change drinking habits by persuading excessive drinkers to give up alcohol. His campaign was credited with administering more than two million pledges to nearly a quarter of the population. Father Cullen's Pioneer Total Abstinence Association concentrated on the young and the sober. The Confirmation pledge was for many years an effective strategy, but by 1970 the Association was said to be concentrating on promoting a sense of responsibility as regards the use of alcohol, encouraging young people to make right decisions about alcohol, its use, abuse, and abstinence. It would be hard to fault this aim, but the evidence points to a doubling of alcohol consumption in Ireland between 1960 and 1980 as prosperity grew, with an increasing intake among the young, especially among women, throughout the 1980s. Less young people now abstain. Underage drinking is widespread and largely ignored. These statistics would surprise nobody who sees the large numbers of predominantly young drinkers thronging the urban pubs throughout the country in 1990. Alongside our increasing consumption has been a parallel rise in all the acknowledged indices of related problems: deaths from liver cirrhosis, admissions to psychiatric hospitals for alcohol abuse, dependence and psychosis, prosecution rates for public drunkenness and for drunken driving. Those who do drink more than compensate in terms of drink-related problems for those who do not.

Despite all of these problems, relative to other countries in Europe Irish consumption of absolute alcohol, estimated per head of population, is still moderate, at approximately eleven litres per year. In France and Luxembourg, where attitudes are over-permissive to alcohol, consumption runs at about twenty litres per capita. Yet the price of alcohol in Ireland, much of it in tax, is one of the highest in Europe, and Ireland has the doubtful distinction of topping the European and possibly the world league table for proportion of disposable income spent on drink, at 11.6 per cent. By comparison, the UK spends only 6.5 per cent of its disposable income on alcoholic beverages, and the US 3.6 per cent. This cannot be good news, in particular for the families of the many Irish who live below the poverty line.

The most obvious drink-related problems stem from intoxication. Irish society has been unusually tolerant of drunkenness — drunks have been more often treated with amused forbearance, at least outside their immediate families, than with stern or outraged disapproval, as occurs in some other societies. Irish drunks are expected to be noisy, boisterous and looking for a fight, a caricature which many have lived up to. This picture of the Irish drunk may have come to the world's attention because of the large number of young male emigrants, dislocated from their homes and suddenly earning quite large sums of money on building sites in the East United States and Britain, where in the 1950s and 1960s they were rather cynically known as 'McAlpine's Fusiliers'.

That such excessive drinking with pugnacious results is not exclusive to the Irish is apparent in recent years in British soccer hooliganism, and is also illustrated by a quote from Maurice Craig's book, *Dublin 1660–1860*. In describing the building of the Custom House he writes: 'Every available mason in Dublin was engaged in the work but such a vast undertaking needed even more labour than was available. Some English carpenters and stonecutters were invited over; "they were very orderly at first", Gandon tells us, "but in the end more refractory than the natives, more exorbitant in their demands for increase of wages, and worse by far as to drunkenness".' The Irish, however, are still seen from other countries to be heavy drinkers, and many Irish writers and artists have revelled in alcohol, perpetuating the image. Flann O'Brien with his pint of plain and Brendan Behan, drinking, talking and singing, come to mind, men who valued their drink, but who also suffered from it.

Excessive drinking, of course, also affects muscular reaction and coordination by the brain, with truly devastating effects on our roads. An Irish study in 1986 found that 67 per cent of people dying in road traffic accidents, pedestrians as well as drivers, passengers and motor-cyclists, contained more than the legal limit of alcohol in the blood. There are many more people seriously injured in motor accidents, leading to extensive hospital care, permanent disability, loss of productivity, and prolonged legal proceedings. Yet we as a society do not shout 'enough', our courts continue to show an alarming proclivity to dismiss drink-related charges on technicalities, and we lag behind most of Europe in allowing our citizens to drive motor vehicles with as much as 80 mgs of alcohol per 100 mls of blood. Even in France the legal limit has been reduced to 50 mgs, while in Sweden the limit is 20 mgs, and in Finland no alcohol at all is permissible in drivers. As the blood alcohol rises, progressively more functions of the brain are affected. Tests have shown that driving skill is certainly affected at 30 mgs and seriously affected by 80 mgs in the blood.

Excessive alcohol intake is all too frequently associated with a litany of other human disasters, to which it contributes mainly by lowering the normal control exerted on behaviour by higher brain centres: suicide and non-fatal deliberate self-harm, crimes against the person, family violence, sexual abuse, including incest, and many unwanted pregnancies are all facilitated by alcohol. At a lesser degree of severity, heavy drinking results in much absenteeism and loss of work efficiency, in the boardroom as much as on the shop floor.

It is difficult to overestimate the amount of distress and psychiatric disability which results in a family where a parent drinks excessively. Certainly some families or individual family members emerge relatively unscathed emotionally, but there is much evidence for emotional and conduct disorders in childhood and adolescence, and for personality disorders, adjustment difficulties, anxiety and depression in later life among family members resulting from prolonged heavy drinking by a parent. Repeated violence to spouses and children, financial insecurity, job loss and acute social embarrassment are all interwoven in such households. But probably most bewildering of all for a growing child are the rapidly changing moods of both its parents, the inconsistent behaviour, the broken promises, with the deceits and pretence to the world that all of this represents normal family life. 'The children haven't suffered' is a hollow claim by many an alcoholic parent.

I have avoided until now the term 'alcoholism' or 'alcoholic', while talking of excessive, heavy and problem drinking. My purpose in so doing has been to emphasise the fact that serious social and medical problems can result from taking a few drinks or even one drink too many, without making the assumption that the drinker is an accustomed heavy drinker who is addicted to alcohol. Again, I would point to the very narrow line between 'moderate' and 'excessive' drinking on any one occasion, which is partly a property of the drug.

But when we consider long-term effects of excessive drinking on the family and also the numerous individual medical and psychiatric conditions resulting from prolonged heavy drinking, then we are moving to think about serious disorders which many professionals rate as diseases, covered by the umbrella term, alcoholism. The term defies precise definition, but in general alcoholism is diagnosed when excessive drinking is associated with deterioration in physical and mental health or in social or personal functioning. Alcoholism is a disputed concept, and different concerned professional groups seek to explain persistent heavy and damaging drinking in ways satisfying their own theoretical bases. In this way sociologists point to social and cultural factors which encourage heavy drinking in society and which render certain groups particularly vulnerable in this respect. Some clinical psychologists emphasise faulty learning of social and also bodily cues which normally enable individuals to know when moderation is being exceeded. Others may consider intrapsychic and interpersonal factors which lead the individual on a path of self-destruction. The supporters of Alcoholics Anonymous, a very helpful organisation, see alcoholism as a disease over which the alcoholic has no control, that he is different from other drinkers and this is usually manifest from the time he takes his first drink. The brewers and distillers like this approach also, as it suggests their products do little harm except in a modest number of abnormal individuals. Governments may favour this interpretation too, as they can provide for a few treatment facilities and continue to collect the enormous revenues from excise duty and VAT which alcohol provides: over £726 million in 1989 in Ireland. This staggering figure represented almost 10 per cent of our total tax revenue last year. Psychiatric medicine views alcoholism both as a behaviour disorder and as a disease, much as coronary heart disease results in part from faulty diet and exercise patterns, and chronic bronchitis from cigarette smoking.

Hospital medicine sees the tip of the alcoholic iceberg, the individuals who have most severely damaged their stomach, intestines, liver, pancreas, heart, peripheral nerves and brain. Some cases of high blood pressure, of throat and colon cancer, and of bone marrow impairment are also attributed to the toxic effects of alcohol. Incredibly, Irish physicians and surgeons record only 0.6 per cent of hospital inpatient admissions as due primarily to the effects of alcohol, while questionnaire screening studies of general medical inpatients and of emergency admissions to Dublin hospitals have found that 15 to 22 per cent scored in the alcoholic range. In our own study, one in three males below the age of sixty-five in general medical wards in Dublin had at some time had serious problems relating to their drinking. These figures complement the few community surveys in Ireland which demonstrate a large amount of undeclared or undetected problem drinking. Recent figures suggest that 11 per cent of adult men and 3 per cent of adult women in the community are currently drinking sufficiently to excess to cause significant problems, and this compares unfavourably with England and Wales, where the figures are 5.3 per cent of men and 1.6 per cent of women.

Some of the most devastating effects of alcohol excess are on the brain. In 1810 Dr William Saunders Hallaran reported that 12 per cent of admissions to the Cork Lunatic Asylum were due to excessive drinking. For some years in the 1970s and 1980s alcoholism and alcoholic psychoses formed the commonest reason for admission to psychiatric hospital, at 25 per cent of all admissions, ahead of depression and schizophrenia. With reducing numbers of hospital beds available, the increasing cost of hospitalisation and shifts in treatment strategies, attitudes have hardened against admitting alcoholics. Treatment in the public health services at least is shifting to outpatient care, with questionable benefit to the alcoholic and his family.

Psychiatry has been trying to find more precise terms with which to categorise damaging drinking. The latest attempt by the World Health Organisation is an improvement on the vague and unsatisfactory term, alcoholism. In its latest International Classification of Diseases (ICD 10) the WHO identifies three syndromes of use of alcohol: 'hazardous use', 'harmful use' and the 'alcohol dependence syndrome' — in old terms 'addiction'.

Running through these syndromes, 'hazardous use' has been delineated by the Royal College of Psychiatrists with reference to a unit of alcohol, consisting of approximately 9 grams of pure alcohol. One unit is contained in a half-pint glass of beer, lager or stout, a glass of wine, a glass of sherry, or a single measure of spirits. 'Hazardous use' is entered when a man regularly drinks more than 21 units in a week, and when a woman drinks regularly more than 14 units in a week. In other words, a man drinking more than 10½ pints a week regularly is taking a risk with his health; a woman drinking more than 7 pints or 14 vodkas weekly is risking illness, for women have smaller volumes of water throughout the body, leading to relatively higher tissue concentrations per unit consumed. A woman who drinks heavily in pregnancy is putting her baby at risk of small birth weight, certain bodily congenital malformations, and reduced intelligence. The US Surgeon General advises women not to drink at all during pregnancy.

These limits for safe drinking come as a shock to many Irish people, and many, especially younger males, are well into the hazardous category. This advice of the Royal College of Psychiatrists is founded on facts, however, and needs to be much more widely known. People who moderate their drinking correspondingly reduce the risks to their health. The WHO's 'harmful use' goes beyond the hazards and is characterised by a pattern that is already causing medical or psychological ill-effects.

The 'alcohol dependence syndrome' is the diagnosis applied to those who are truly addicted to alcohol:

continuing their supply of alcohol has become their main aim in life, and ordinary reasoning or persuasion can have little effect on their behaviour. They continue to drink despite so many good reasons why they should stop. Family, friends, job and health all take second place. Such addicts, who may be middle-aged mothers as well as young male sociopaths, can tolerate very large quantities of alcohol and may drink throughout the day. But when they stop or sharply reduce their intake they develop withdrawal symptoms: shaking, nervousness, sweating and nausea in mild cases, and often each morning; epileptic fits, mental confusion or the DTs in severe cases. *Delirium tremens* is a serious condition in which the individual is feverish, confused, tremulous, often hallucinated and terrified, and it requires urgent medical treatment.

Alcoholism overall carries two to four times average mortality risk. Thirty per cent of a sample of alcoholics in one Boston study were dead nine years later. Longer term effects in those who survive many years of heavy drinking are particularly severe on the brain and the liver. The memory can be so damaged that a person returning to the room after a couple of minutes may be greeted by the chronic alcoholic as someone he has never met before. A more widespread brain failure, or dementia, is probably more common than we realise, while chronic liver disease is well recognised and a significant cause of death.

One of the remaining questions relating to alcohol in Ireland, only hinted at in this paper, is *why* some people develop harmful and addictive patterns of drinking? The simple answer is because they drink too much, they succumb to the curse of the drinking classes, but, like all glib answers, this is too simple. I have indicated that cultural and social factors have led to an inclination and tolerance for heavy drinking in Ireland. Certain occupational groups have a high incidence of alcoholism, in particular, publicans and bartenders, entertainers and journalists, armed service personnel, salesmen and doctors.

Prospective longitudinal research has identified particularly three factors which distinguish those who become
alcoholic from those who do not: a family history of
alcoholism; belonging to an ethnic group which tolerates
drunkenness; and a pre-existing pattern of anti-social
behaviour, for example, school problems and truancy.
From studies in the US and in Scandinavia there is now
convincing evidence that genetic factors predispose some
people to alcoholism, at least in males. And children who
have short attention spans and are hyperactive may carry
an increased risk. There are, then, a host of predisposing
causes for harmful and addictive drinking which may be
summed up by reference to the constitution of the
individual, his family and social setting and the availability
of the drug alcohol.

Can we alter the present awful situation relating to
damage and distress with which alcohol is associated in
Ireland? In retrospect, the West seems to have chosen the
wrong recreational drug, but the alternatives are not too
reliable either. Prohibition in the West did not work.
Probably a good deal could be achieved by firm controls
on price, retail outlets and advertising, but these issues are
complex, and restrictions will be opposed by very powerful
economic and employment lobbies. Immediate improvement in the amount of death and damage could result from
the implementation of stronger restrictions on drinking
and driving. Educational efforts have been under-funded
feeble and unfocussed, but continued and determined stress
on the need for abstinence or moderation, and avoidance of
excess, will help to shift public attitudes, much as they have
begun to change in relation to smoking. We need also early
preventive efforts among those at risk, and effective detection and treatment for those who have already damaged
their own health and that of their family. A comprehensive
national plan on alcohol is needed, and this at a time when
the Irish National Council on Alcoholism has had to
disband because of withdrawal of central support.

George Vaillant's book, *The Natural History of Alcoholism*, opens with the following arresting paragraph:

> Alcoholism is a disorder of great destructive power. Depending on how one defines alcoholism, it will afflict, at some time in their lives, between 3 and 10 per cent of all Americans. In the United States alcoholism is involved in a quarter of all admissions to general hospitals, and it plays a major role in the four most common causes of death in males aged 20–40: suicide, accidents, homicide, and cirrhosis of the liver. The damage it causes falls not only on alcoholics themselves but on their families and friends as well — and this damage touches one American family out of three.

In Ireland we should not continue to ignore such information. Although moderate drinking in sensible settings does seem to suit us, we have yet to solve the curse of the drinking classes: excessive drinking. *Sláinte!*

TEN

A Future for our Mentally Ill?

Charles Smith

A few years ago I was asked to write a chapter on the history of the Central Mental Hospital, Dundrum, for a forensic psychiatry textbook. The hospital has an intact set of records dating back to its opening in 1850 and I was intrigued to discover that its problems in the last century were not terribly different from its difficulties now in the late twentieth century. For example, my predecessors then worried about and bemoaned the fact that the hospital was overcrowded, that staff/patient ratios were too low, that security was easily breached and that the attendants were increasingly challenging of medical authority. They complained of the influx of dangerous prisoners from the ordinary prison system and of the pressure to move out the less disturbed and more predictable working patients in the hospital. Real change comes slowly, and organisations such as hospitals, and security hospitals in particular, have what a former Reith lecturer, Dr Schon, described as inherent, namely 'dynamic conservatism'. Psychiatry is part of a traditionally slow-moving and slow-changing system and currently it is being pushed or pulled into a future that it is very uncertain of. If history is anything to go by, psychiatry is quite likely to end up with less change than was planned because that seems to be the nature of the art. I was talking recently to an administrative colleague who told me that he had been involved with others in producing a position paper on mental handicap over ten years ago. They highlighted the need then for almost exactly the

same number of residential places identified as a requirement
by a report that surfaced in 1988. He advised that if you
stand in the same place events will circle round to greet
you in cycles. All too true.

We spend approximately 16 per cent of the total health
non-capital budget on matters psychiatric. That compares
with similar proportions of public expenditure in other
Western systems, but, considering the high proportions of
psychiatric patients in the total patient population it does
seem and feel like under-funding. There must be good
reason for this and it is worth a little bit of conjecture.
Obviously, psychiatric patients are troubled enough by
what is going on inside themselves to be rendered less
capable of organising effectively what goes on outside.
Illness is a self-consuming process. Pain, emotional or
physical, is very self centring and it leaves little time to get
concerned about broader social or political issues. Patients
simply cannot organise as consumers. It is left then largely
to the professionals who try to care for them or redirect
them to act for them, but, unfortunately, I do not think
that psychiatry is good at representing the patient in its
care or representing itself too well either. This is partly
because psychiatry is a many-splintered thing, with groups
such as the Irish Division of the Royal College, the Irish
Medical Organisation, a national organisation of Clinical
Directors, regional organisations of Consultants and a
single organisation of non-Consultant psychiatric trainees.
This organisational chaos is counter productive and it fails
to protect or project the carers and the cared for.

I think the problem has been one of passivity as well, a
passivity that borders on the pathological. I feel it has
something to do with the training that prepares one for
psychiatry, during which inevitably and inexorably one gets
better at shipping criticism and insult and angry outbursts,
without over-reacting in the first place, and eventually without reacting at all. The usual comment made to psychiatrists
in a social setting is: how on earth can you listen to troubles

all day long and still remain reasonably equable? The answer, of course, is not the over-used one, that psychiatrists don't listen, it is rather that training allows one to be involved in quite an empathic and serviceable way with patients, but it also equips one for dropping the load as soon as the session is over. If the training encourages passivity, and I think it does, it is then very hard to get groups of psychiatrists excited about terms and conditions of living for their patients or terms and conditions of working for themselves. Patients and their carers end up seriously disadvantaged, I would feel, as a consequence. Sometimes it does seem that the loudest public protest grabs most of the resources, and psychiatry is simply not good enough at protesting.

What of current policy and trends in psychiatric practice? The excellent planning document which surfaced through the Department of Health some five or six years ago, simply titled *Planning for the Future*, had worthy aims, and central to these was the dismantling of larger, worn-out institutions and that means, of course, discharging the patients within to some alternative. The process was called communitisation or de-institutionalisation and the intention was that large, unworkable, inhuman institutions would be replaced by care in the community, staying as close as possible to the individual's home of origin and moving him into general district hospitals if a crisis emerged needing inpatient care. Large numbers of residential hostels were planned of varying gradation, using terms like high and low support, and it seemed that the high-support hostels would have high levels of staffing and the low-support hostels would not. It did seem as well that the high-support hostels would be the equivalent of small wards, but that they would be more domestic in character and architecture, more conducive to the restoration of normal dignity and human participation. Nobody could argue with such lofty idealistic planning, although almost every single professional wondered about the high cost of the transitional period, that is, the period that would inevitably exist between the closing-down of the institutions and the opening-up of the new alternatives. It did seem to psychiatrists generally (and they don't have a clue about macroeconomics, I can assure you) that a lot of extra money was needed to put the infrastructure for the new system into place. The hope and the intention for the new era was that the old institutions would close down, the fixed asset would be realised, the staff would vacate into the community and some interim borrowing would cover the gap. It simply has not worked out like that, nor is it likely to.

Let us look at what happens at institutional level. The first third of the patient population can probably be moved on to alternative accommodation and supports with good driving team work and co-operation. There is little doubt about that. That first group of patients can slip almost unnoticed into small hostels that look like ordinary houses. The community hardly notices that they are there and ordinarily they go to sheltered or unsheltered employment during working hours and it is a very real improvement on large institutional living. It gets harder to move on the remaining patients waiting in the aisles, however. Exaggerating just to make the point, the more difficult patients stay behind requiring perhaps even the same number of staff that surrounded the entire complement at an earlier stage and the unit bed costs go up. In simple terms, you have a reduced number of beds without a reduction in costs, and, of course, the cost per bed increases. That does not look so good, so the push continues and, as far as I am concerned, if you keep pushing too far, too quickly, you can end up with the sufferers of what was formerly labelled illness, and treated as such, living in small, soulless hostels. These hostels look very much like the wards the patients vacated in the first place, only smaller in scale or, worse still, some former patients slip through the net altogether to join the wandering homeless who constitute a growing group in most large cities in the Western world.

There is very, very real concern coming from New York, London, Melbourne — anywhere where the planning process was similar — about mental illness on the streets. I am not saying we have reached that stage in Dublin, but I do say that we could arrive there. We are at a crossroads now and we need to stop and read the signposts, to look at what has been achieved with the very good intentions of *Planning for the Future*, what risks have emerged that were not anticipated, what pitfalls are opening up ahead of us or what pitfalls we are actively digging as we push an inadequately funded service, that affects so many individuals and families, toward an uncertain future.

I recently did a tour of the large hostels that have been on site in Dublin for decades. I knew all of them from the time I was in medical school over thirty years ago, but I had never set foot inside any of them. I went to the Iveagh Hostel and up from it at Christchurch into the Backlane. I moved across the river to the Corporation Hostel in Benburb Street (for reasons that are not too clear it is known at the Model) and I ended up at the Morning Star over beside the old Richmond Hospital. To complete the tour I stopped off at a food distribution centre in Church Lane where they turn out 300 dinners a day and I was left with more than an impression that we have quite a substantial problem in these locations. It is not an entirely new problem. It was there long before *Planning for the Future* looked over the parapet, but it is in a critical state. The people who work in those locations tell me that there is a definite shift in their population, particularly in the last couple of years. They continue to house the elderly, but they now have to protect them more so than formerly from a younger, disruptive group that seems both disturbed and substance abusing, and at times downright ill. I would contend that de-institutionalisation has contributed to some extent to this new phenomenon. This younger group formerly had access to the asylum. It doesn't now.

I know that claims are made that we are different from our nearest neighbour: for instance, different in so far as the percentage of hostels in Ireland under health board or local authority control is much higher than in Britain, but we seem to be producing or reproducing the dilemmas that have arisen elsewhere.

I have not even mentioned the substantial numbers of patients who live in rent-supported private accommodation. I only come across a tiny number of them, but the few that I see live very boring and unstimulating lives. I would imagine that they might be better off in the institutional ward where the television was on all the time and growing institutional apathy and indifference awaited those who lingered too long. The Americans have a new term, called 'trans-institutionalisation' and it refers, I think, to the dangers of patients moving from one bad system to another. We have to watch out that we do not go too far down that unhappy road.

Sometime ago I got myself into a bit of trouble by seeming to say that there was a correlation between the reducing psychiatric patient population and the increasing prison population. Correlations are very different from causations and I am not really making such a link, but I do know a little bit about what is going on in the prison system and, talking to colleagues who work there and staff who work there, and having worked there myself over many years, I am worried that there is a risk that uncared-for illness may end up very inappropriately in a prison setting. Illness abandoned is illness at risk.

As for the psychiatric units in the general hospitals, these were part of the new era as well. As far as I know, they are working effectively in Galway and Cork and in St James's Hospital in Dublin. There is a good functioning unit in St Vincent's Hospital in Dublin, but it does not accept catchment area responsibility as intended in *Planning for the Future*, so I see it as somewhat different from the other three and I know that there certainly has been delay if not lack of interest in setting up the units in both the Mater Hospital and Beaumont. I have to admit that I might be wrong about this assumption, but I think I am on to a safe wicket because I can well understand it. I can understand the reluctance of a general hospital to have an active psychiatric unit with a full catchment area of responsibility operating within its walls. I can understand the concern about disruptive illness milling around in casualty, there is probably enough there already. (As an aside, I am often asked about the dangers that surround working in a place like the Central Mental Hospital, Dundrum. I am regarded as either a fool or a saint at risk and I usually respond by saying that there is far more danger of personal injury in a busy casualty department on a Saturday night. Dundrum has lots of minor incidents, but very few major ones. It is a very safe place to work, paradoxically.)

The idea of the general hospital units is a good one; integrate psychiatry, make it as akin to general medicine as possible, house it on the same campus — but it is not that simple. So another cornerstone of the planning has to be looked at again. I still think it is achievable, but it is not 'acheapable'. These better systems — good community care and good general hospital psychiatric units — need good funding, good public support, good professional co-operation.

Let me move on to professional co-operation, and I am confining myself to the professionals who work in and around the Psychiatric Service. There is growing disenchantment with traditional claimed medical leadership. Psychologists as a professional group are now almost free of medical interference, close to professional independence and more power to them. Social workers working in hospitals may resent medical leadership, but they do not resign over it as far as I can see, not that they are resigned to it. Nurses, the traditional medical allies, are quite strident now in their criticism of medical flaunting and power grabbing.

In the past doctors were allowed this leadership role almost as a birthright, and of course they are not going to hold on to it in the future unless they deserve to lead. I am not sure what the process of change will involve or how many heads will roll, but I think that doctors and nurses will probably end up closer to each other than to the other groups.

What about administration? Hospital administrators are the new power group because power lies where the money lies, and while the Department of Finance controls funds these pass through the Department of Health and through administrative fingers before reaching treatment locations. Recent figures reveal that administrative staffing at all levels has increased at a time when other staff groupings have suffered losses during the recession. There is probably good reason for it, but it is not too obvious to this reviewer, at least. We are beginning to notice the emergence of a professional administrative leadership, but there is far too little of it around and it takes a long time to grow. Professional administration can cause a lot of problems, particularly if the office holders are resentful of medical power and want to cut it down to size simply to show that there has been a power shift. Certainly, bad medical leadership should be challenged but good leadership should be allowed its head. I think a lot of administrators operate with a hidden agenda, and I have become convinced that a small core group of administrators here link up with a similar core group in the British NHS and plan, not the dismantling of institutions, but the dismantling of the psychiatric staff. I do not know much about administration. I am resentful when it thinks it knows all about psychiatry. I said earlier that psychiatry and nursing may close ranks. I would love to see a real reduction in tension between psychiatry and administration. It just may be in the patients' interest that suspicion and distancing are replaced by mutual acknowledgment of each group's pivotal value and contribution.

I cannot understand the survival of health boards as currently constituted. I have only seen one health board in operation, through attending a few meetings of the Eastern Health Board and, of course, sitting in on visiting sub-committees from the parent board involved at my base hospital. I know that it is all part of the democratic process and that there are arguments in favour of wide representation, public accountability and all of that. However, it does seem to me that there are downside weaknesses and risks. There are political manoeuvrings and groupings and strategies that can interfere with cohesive work and decision making. It may be unfair, but I think that health boards are quite politicised, with young careers lifting off and older careers languishing for a while before oblivion. That is perhaps a little unkind and it fails to acknowledge the positive side of the individual investment: health boards obviously attract and retain many socially committed altruistic individuals and it seems silly to denigrate anything that includes such worthy ideals. However, from a work functioning point of view it is my impression that health boards are too large, too disparate, too fragmented, to offer cohesive intention and policy. I would replace them, if I could, with something much smaller, something that looks more like the board of a commercial company with three or four executive directors and a similar number of non-executive directors chosen for their talents and their likely contributions. The decisions and workings of that board would not go on in public. It would not have to look over its shoulder all of the time or manoeuvre politically. It should have some chance of managing a vast organisation with large amounts of money shifting around within that service system. It might be open to some terrible scandal in so far as its decisions would not be in the public glare, but I think the risk is worth taking.

There is a need to update the 1945 Mental Treatment Act. It has served us well and it was very nearly replaced by the Health (Mental Services) Act 1981. That legislation was passed by the Dáil and the Senate, it got the Presidential imprimatur, but it was not signed into law by the Minister. It had a lot to recommend it, despite some shortcomings. I am not sure why it faltered in its final phase, but I do know that the Department of Health is now actively reviewing the whole topic. The Department has been convincingly consultative during this process and I think we can anticipate new legislation soon. I do not envy the task of those who will draft the legislation. It is an enormously complicated process to attempt to cater for changing individual and societal needs, to change requirements and obligations, and it goes without saying that legislation can be tightened up to the point where there is no flexibility in a system that requires room to manoeuvre. However, there are some basic principles, and if these are acknowledged and incorporated in new legislation we will certainly be on the right road. They emanate from a UN Committee, no less, and date back to 1983.

These principles assert that patients are entitled to the least restrictive environment when ill, to privacy and dignity, legal protection and appeal process. They should have rights to communicate freely, to visitors and uncensored mail. They should have the right to practise their religion and to exercise all civil, political, social and cultural rights, including the management of their own affairs. They should have the right to educational, vocational and recreational inputs, and the right to qualified guardianship, including legal aid. In a broad sense they should not be exposed to exploitation or experimentation. Clearly, these well thought-out principles protect the consumer and, of course, they cannot be ignored. The core difficulties are those involving detention of illness and the review of that detention. There can be a conflict between rights to freedom and rights to treatment, and I do not imagine for one minute that all of these dilemmas will be resolved in every case, it is simply impossible. All that one can attempt to do is rectify most wrongs and reduce most errors.

Removing freedom, even in the cause of treatment, has to be regarded as an extremely serious decision, as serious or more serious even than an arrest process, and it must be statutorily reviewed. In other words, the legality of the detention and the requirement of detention must be reviewed to make sure that both are in order. Within the UN guidelines treatment locations will obviously be dignified and humane and professionally staffed. Treatment should be participative, acknowledging the value of informed consent. I am not too sure that we are capable of arriving at these destinations and I am reassured by the growing interest of the European Commission in places of detention. That obviously includes prisons and security hospitals, but it can extend to psychiatric hospitals as well. The European Court, as final arbiter, has judged appeals from detained patients, and I think we can expect more individual or class actions played out in the European arena unless we move energetically in the right direction. While I am, quite rightly I think, focussing on the process of detention and the problems surrounding it, knowing that it is a real concern for existing and future patients, nevertheless I do not think it is going to be a major issue or as big an issue in the future. Seeing a number of my senior colleagues trying to locate a bed for an emergency admission, I realise that the patient of the future may have more difficulty getting into hospital than getting out of it.

Before ending I would like to touch on the need for our institutions to open up to the public gaze and scrutiny. In the Central Mental Hospital, Dundrum, over the last several years we have encouraged more visiting from professionals, students, interested lay groups, and we have run, almost to the point of boring our colleagues, several professional conferences, all partly with the aim of letting more people see what goes on behind our high walls. I would like, if it were possible, to have an open day in a place like Dundrum, and on that theme it is interesting to recall, without revealing the individual's name, a conversation that I had recently with a prison governor. I was remarking on the access that television cameras and crews seem to have into English and Scottish prisons. I saw a BBC team in the depths of Peterhead Prison in Scotland actually interviewing an inmate on a dirty protest. Now while that may seem healthily open it could be quite tricky in a particular case. One wonders about the capacity of an individual so distressed to give valid consent for an interview. Nevertheless, I thought the openness was mostly helpful. The prison governor and I were agreeing that we are nominally in charge of institutions of society that society knows little about. We appeal to society for support. We aim at informing but we worry about reforming. He and I would argue that society is responsible for its prisons, its hospitals, its hostels, and that it cannot face that responsibility unless it is informed. I am not at all convinced that society is particularly interested, to be honest, and I can understand part of that response. A few years ago a friend stayed with me for a weekend and it took me some time to appreciate that he was quite changed and quite abnormal. I quickly strategised his return home to Scotland, setting up treatment and support there, but I was quite aware of a rejecting process. I was quite keen to move responsibility for him elsewhere and I think on a broader front society is still capable of similar rejection. Quite recently there was substantial publicity surrounding an attempt to open a hostel for handicapped individuals in some Dublin location and it was strenuously resisted with the usual arguments about falling house prices, etc. That type of protest increases when attempts are made to open hostels for prisoners or to find locations for open prisons, and we might as well acknowledge it as a late twentieth-century reality.

In some ways I am finishing this chapter on a pessimistic note. There are many problems within the treatment systems. Various professional groups are sorting out territories. In rapidly changing times there is growing distrust between first-line treatment personnel and administrators, and I think as well that the health boards that I criticised earlier are unhappy with attempts to reduce their autonomy. When that is combined with a society that has lost its traditional tolerance and caring interest we suddenly have quite a major task on our hands. I hope we have the energy and the charity to sort it all out.

Index

strokes, 67
suicide, 18–30
    Christian attitude to, 19–21
    historically, 18–20
    legal sanctions against, 21, 25
    and mental illness, 21–4, 26, 30,
        88, 95–7
    parasuicide, 26–7
    programme to combat, 28–30
    public attitudes to, 30
    statistics, 5, 18, 24–5, 29, 95
Suicide Act, 1961 (UK), 21
Sweden, 104
Swift, Jonathan, 63
Switzerland, 29

Temperance Movement, 63, 102
trans-sexualism, 58–9
transvestites, 59

unemployment, 92
United Kingdom
    Black Report, 46
    community care, 116, 117
    homicide studies, 81
    hospital administration, 119
    insanity defence, 83–4
    mental hospitals, 69
    power of attorney, 75
    prison system, 123
    study of sexual disorder, 61–3
    suicide legislation, 21
    use of alcohol, 101, 102, 103,
        104, 107

United States of America, 24
    community care, 116, 117
    studies of education, 48
    studies of homicide, 81
    studies of schizophrenia, 34–6
    study of sexual dysfunction, 55–6
    use of alcohol, 103, 108, 109,
        110, 111

vaginismus, 56, 61–2
Vaillant, George, 111
voyeurism, 59–60

Waddington, David, 13
Walsh, Dr Dermot, 6
ward of court, 74–5
Wilde, Lady, 33
Wilde, Oscar, 100
Woolf, Virginia, 91
World Health Organisation (WHO),
    18, 108

*Years Ahead, The — A Policy for the
    Elderly*, 70
Yeats, W.B., 15, 21, 41